CW00985546

VOICES
FROM
THE DARK

VOICES
FROM
THE DARK

By

ALAN S BELLINGER

CENTRAL PUBLISHING LIMITED
West Yorkshire

Paperback ISBN 1 903970 73 3

Published
by

Central Publishing Limited
Royd Street Offices
Milnsbridge
Huddersfield
West Yorkshire
HD3 4QY

www.centralpublishing.co.uk

Voices From The Dark

The Making of a Spiritual Healer

"The time has come" the walrus said "to talk of many things, of candlesticks and sealing wax and Cabbages and Kings" Omar Khayam.

Many friends and acquaintances as well as patients have been telling me for some years that I should stop boring them with repetitions of my experiences and instead write a book. They may have a point – and I will do my best to record some of the more interesting events in what has been a fairly long and interesting life. I will dedicate it to the many souls unseen who have guided me through many different and difficult problems.

I was born on the 26th September 1913 in Havelock Square, Sheffield. Many years later it was to become the centre of the Red Light Area and the scene of the activities of a multiple killer called Peter Sutcliffe –'The Yorkshire Ripper'.

Both my parents had been born in the Lake District, Cumberland. Mother was the only child of Granny Kerr (nee Rothery) the daughter of a well to do Master Grocer of Cockermouth. She had fallen in love with a John Kerr, son and heir I believe of a Scottish Lord from the borders of Scotland. They became engaged but broke off this arrangement because she fell out with his gambling, shooting, fishing type of life. However they kept each others presents and she kept the ring. Subsequently they could not resist each other, Granny relented, and they became engaged again. Granny always wore two engagement rings! From the same man!

After Mother was born in Workington, where Granny had investment property, Granny again fell out with John over his lifestyle. She offered to pay off his gambling debts for the last time and give him £500 if he undertook to leave England and never come back. He accepted and joined the Canadian Mounties. He could ride and shoot and it qualified him for this exciting life.

Much later he was engaged in the Boxer war in China and was killed – possibly by drowning in the Yangtsee River. In a BBC TV programme in the early 1990's on this subject, the camera showed the graves in the English War cemetery and showed as its last shot the individual grave of John Kerr, my grandfather. The BBC said they could not let me have a video of the programme as it was not theirs!! (They did offer to show it to me in their studios in London for £80, but I would not be able to take a copy, so I did not pursue it).

My mother was related to William Wordsworth, the poet, and when their first born turned out to be a girl they received requests from the Wordsworth society, that she should be named 'Dorothy Wordsworth Bellinger' and that is what they did; two years later I arrived.

Father was the son of a Frederick Bellinger who had a large family of nine children. He and my father worked in Workington at the Cammell Llaird Iron works. My father constantly tried to educate himself so that he could leave this hard life. Before he left he did become the works champion wrestler in 'Catch-as-Catch-Can' wrestling so he must have been quite strong physically. He left this work and became an insurance salesman and eventually came to Sheffield where he was employed by the Commercial Union Insurance Company, and that is how I came to be born there, rather than in the Lake District

When his wages permitted and I was about three years old, we moved to the outer suburbs of Nether Edge, west side of Sheffield and very close at that time to the very beautiful countryside that surrounds the industrial city; where I can remember quite clearly items that occurred from the age of two to three. It was a semi-detached stone built rented house; number 80, Nether Edge Road. There was a long garden with an earth closet at the bottom of it. We kept poultry and later pigeons. Their droppings created the finest liquid manure for mother's sweet peas which grew close by. There was a lean-to summer house against the end wall over which I could scramble into the next garden where my friend Jackie Batt lived.

Early photographs show me as a very fair-haired, boisterous boy and I can remember that there was an asphalted kitchen yard. I am told I was playing there with a wooden train while my grandfather (FB) was trying to sleep in a deck chair. He told me roughly to 'stop it'. Apparently I did not like his peremptory tone, picked up my engine and 'crowned' him with it. Fortunately my father was in the garden, heard the fracas and was just in time to save me from retribution!

One of the incidents I remember from that time, concerned the cellar which was approached from within the kitchen. On opening the cellar door you were confronted with a descending set of stone steps which turned a 90 degree turn to the right immediately from the top. There were no lights in this stairwell, nor in the cellar below, which contained the coal supply. I was very curious as to how deep it was and tried to assess the depth by throwing down a tea cup to check on the time it took to hit the bottom! Just as it crashed, mother came into the kitchen and heard the noise. She asked me what I had done – so I told her. She explained that I had not to throw cups down the cellar steps because they would break and of course I agreed not to do it again. She then went out of the kitchen to do her housework. When she returned, it was to the sound of something else crashing into the cellar. She again asked me what I had thrown down. I told her I had not thrown a cup, only a saucer! She then patiently told me not to throw anything down which would break. She next heard the cat meowing from the dark depths and I had to explain that it would not break. So very logical to my child mind!

I was the second child of six and I can remember seeing the search-lights and the Zeppelin which came over the city during the First Great War which started in 1914. I can remember that sometime later, my father was called up for a medical, prior to conscription, in spite of having some claim to a special job (I believe he was by now a Chief Clerk with responsibilities in the Commercial Union Insurance Company; and I can remember that he worked long hours at home studying for his exams). I can remember his return from the medical examination for conscription (compulsory call-up) *overjoyed* that he had been rejected on the grounds of poor eyesight and possibly a heart condition.

At the end of the war when the Armistice was declared my father took me to Sheffield City Centre, on the Moor to see the celebrations. The Moor (a central main street in the city) was full of rejoicing people and there were tanks being shown off and I remember being allowed to touch some of the levers attached to the rear of one of these gigantic vehicles.

When I was about 4½ years old I started attending a small private school, which was Miss Jackson's, at the bottom of Nether Edge Road in Sharrow Lane. I can still remember the songs they taught me in French. I also remember the embarrassment I suffered whenever I had to use the toilet. I wore short grey trousers held up by braces. Because I released the two back braces buttons first, that part shot up behind my neck and after I had finished and buttoned the front both sides buttons, I could not reach the back ones which were by then behind my neck. So for the rest of that period until I went home I had to keep my pants up by having my hands in my pockets!

After about a year, when I was five, I contracted TB and suffered tubercular glands in the neck; possibly from the untreated cow's milk we had in those days. By that time I had a younger brother Laurence – but neither he nor Dorothy were affected as I was.

Mother was a Christian Scientist and was against surgery and medical drugs etc. So after I was confirmed as having the problem I had no medicine only bed rest and lots of TLC. I can remember mother encouraging me to "eat it all up" when she brought a tray to my bed, if I did I might even live to be 30 years old. She called upon the Christian Scientists to send a 'Thinker' (what I believe we would now term a Healer). He was a Mr Sinnam; he was dressed very formally in dark pin-stripe trousers, wing collar and black jacket. He sat at my bedside, put his head on his right hand with elbow supported on my bed, and did his 'Thinking'. He must have been a healer because I got better; though I can remember mother was still wheeling me about in a pram (pushchair type) when I was seven years old.

When I was well enough, I attended Carter Knowle School on Bannerdale Road, which was some two miles away. I remember suddenly feeling as though the scales had been taken from in front of my eyes and it all began to make sense. I became an avid reader and did very well in class, climbing rapidly towards the top. We walked in those days and went home for lunch as well. Quite often I would have to run an errand for essential food for lunch down to Nether Edge Terminus, I became a very fast runner – otherwise there would have been no time to eat!

At that school I was frequently bullied because of my frail appearance. It was only when my temper flared and I attacked my tormentors that I was suddenly accepted and was no longer a butt for their torments.

It was about this time that my mother was taken ill and father brought in the doctor who diagnosed acute appendicitis and said that she would have to have an operation. Mother said she would not have the operation and told them to leave her with me. After they had left she told me to put my hands on her tummy and stroke her over the site of the appendix. She got better without further need to call the doctor (perhaps she knew instinctively that I could heal – a hint of what was to come in the future).

At about that time I had a very vivid dream. It made such an impression that I told it to my mother who promptly said she knew what that meant. She said it indicated that I would one day travel to the Holy Land and see all the important sites in the life of Jesus of Nazareth. In the dream I had seen a short oak stave or walking stick suddenly sprout wings and fly. In the Second Great War I was posted to the Palestine area with the 1st Cavalry Division and at one time we camped at the foot of the Mount of Sacrifice. This I climbed several times to the monastery at its crest. The monks there treated me very well and gave me food and drink. On one of my visits, they told me that it would be my last visit to see them, they offered me an oaken stave as a memento that they had cut from a stunted oak that grew on the mountain. They gave me a choice of one which was five feet long or one which was less than three feet long. I chose the smaller as it would fit into my kit-bag. I still have this memento today. (see account later in War experiences).

Three days later I was seconded to Brigade Head Quarters at Sarafand where I set up a huge transit camp under the command of a Major Hugh McTavish. He was a personal friend of General Wavell (dating from the 1st Great War). It was he who gave me passes to travel all around Palestine when leave was possible. He had also armed me with a permit to carry a camera and take photographs. This enabled me to visit the Holy Places which I had not seen while with the Cavalry Regiment. Thus mother's interpretation of my dream came true in every detail.

When I was about 10½ years old mother took us all (5 children) to her mother's (Granny Kerr). I was never told anything other than the fact that mother was running away from father. No reason was given to us children. Granny recommended that we should disappear for some time and the best place would be Northern Ireland. She must have provided mother with the necessary money and we sailed from Liverpool to Belfast. From there we took the train to travel north to Rathmullen on Lough Swilly.

We put up at a small hotel and assumed the name of Robinson. This change of name led to some funny situations, for instance, we were playing hide-and-seek about the Hotel; Joyce saw Connie in her hidey hole and shouted out 'I spy you Connie Bellinger'. We were instantly shocked and retreated rapidly to our bedrooms.

In Rathmullen the Mail Driver brought goods as well as letters to the hotel. For this he was given a daily lunch which consisted of potatoes baked in their skins + water, salt and butter. They were piled high on a large plate and he bit into them as one would eating an apple. I counted hem one day. He ate 19 potatoes.

After nine months we all returned and I had missed taking my 11 plus exam for entry to Grammar school. Father made special representations to the Education Department and won permission for me to take the entrance exam, and I passed. My grade was sufficient to get me to Firth Park Grammar School or to a planned new Grammar School at Nether edge. As the latter was within walking distance of home we chose that, as Firth Park was a long tram ride away at the other side of Sheffield. Because this new school was late in opening, the first intake of scholars had only three years and one term, instead of the usual four years in which to take the Matriculation exam. At this school I was near the top in the top class, either 2nd or 3rd. Usually Ron Spathaky was 1st (and also Victor Ludorum) and Eric Brown was 2nd. I was the first school chess champion. I even beat the physics master who dealt with chess.

At this time I was an avid reader of everything. I was most impressed by 'The Count of Monte Christo' by Alexander Dumas. *'The priest who was in the next cell to our hero taught him the skill of withdrawing from the body and 'astral travelling'.* I learnt how to do it too, and was thereby convinced, at that early age, that I was of spirit. I asked 'them' to leave me and let me deal with this material life and 'they' did this, except for the odd prophetic dream etc., until I neared retirement. Then it developed rapidly through the catalyst of John's illness.

I had an elder sister born 1911, Dorothy Wordsworth, a brother Laurence Hartley arrived two years after me, then there was a pause to be followed by first Joyce and then Constance Lillian. Some years after rejoining my father, Hazel was born. Mother at first thought and hoped it was indigestion!

Mother had great faith in me and I was always the first to bathe the new born baby (always at home without problems); Joyce 19th November, 1918, 11lbs, and then Connie 29th January, 1920, 12lbs, were very large babies; Hazel put in an appearance on 17th July 1926 at 14lbs She looked about six months old at birth! She grew up as the constant companion of her two elder sisters and made the same academic progress. So at three years of age she could read and write fluently and as well as her sisters. At the age of seven she wrote and produced a simple play for her little friends to enact, it was called 'The Red Hand Gang'. When Hazel sat her 11 plus exam to qualify for Grammar school education she was nine years old and she came 9th in all Sheffield, but she was still a baby in many ways to me.

When I first arrived at the Nether Edge Grammar School I found that we were all to be medically examined. The doctor said that I had a murmur of the heart and would therefore be unable to take part in games of any sort. However, I felt alright and proceeded to play football, cricket and the full schedule in the gymnasium. I found that I could kick equally well with either foot and I enjoyed all these activities.

From being a very good copper-plate hand writer I soon learned that it had to be the fastest writing that mattered in order to get down all the notes that we had to take. So I was soon one of the fastest writers in the class, trouble was, I could hardly read it. My best subject was physics, but I was fairly good at all five or six subjects.

The first headmaster had been a Mr Ritchings but after a year or so he went elsewhere and Mr Harold Smith took over, he had been a master for English at the Public School of St. Bees in Cumberland. When we came to sit the finals for the Matriculation he was invigilating over my class when I had to ask to go urgently, to the toilet. He gave permission and was somewhat surprised, shortly after to hear me bellowing 'I can't get out'. The toilet door had jammed; the door opened inwards; and I could not open it. He heard my shouts and

10

came to my assistance. Stand clear he said and gave the door a mighty kick and it yielded and I was released. Thirty years after, when I was back at Fitzalan Square, I attended an open day at the school which by then had been re-sited in new premises. When he saw me he recalled the embarrassing moment and told me that I was one of the school's success stories.

Among my group of school friends we all said what we would like to do for a living. I told them that I would like to be a doctor. However I did not win a scholarship to university and my father said he could not afford to send me to University and that he had got me a position in a bank, just what I said was my last choice.

One of father's business/golfing friends was the manager of the High Street branch of Barclays Bank and so I went for tests and interview and got the job. The Bank had a rule that all staff had to be medically 'A1' and have vaccinations against smallpox. This latter was something my father had always objected to – even when it entailed a court appearance and registering as a Conscientious Objector. However, for this situation he raised no objection and I was duly vaccinated. Within a very short time I started having migraine headaches in a severe form and I always felt that this was the true cause. I also got myself a doctor under the National Health and asked him if my heart had a murmur. He tested me very carefully and said that in his opinion I could not have had one in the past, so much for the school doctor and all those years of worrying!

My first position in the Bank was to the Chesterfield Branch and it was the 13th October 1930. I always had the feeling that number 13 was my lucky number and it kept cropping up as though to prove it. My numerology number is 4 and I was told by a Medium that my Spiritual number is 9 = 13. My starting salary was £50.00 per annum paid monthly. There was an automatic pension at age sixty, calculated by your number of year's service over sixty and in my case that was 43/60. Later they reduced it to two thirds of finishing salary.

Another rule was that you had to have the Bank's permission to get married and this could not be until you were earning £250.00 per annum. If, heaven forbid, you HAD to get married, then your parents had to guarantee to make up the salary to the sum of £250.00. There was no deduction from the salary for the pension. The Bank put in a certain proportion of the total salary bill into a Pension Fund which was managed by Bank Trustees. There were concessionary rates of interest; you were not allowed to overdraw; borrowing had to be specially sanctioned and taken on loan account and there were special rules to help in the purchase of a house; no smoking was allowed when the Bank was open to the public.

The manager of the Chesterfield Branch was a Mr Hudson and he was a very kind, thoughtful and gentle person. He advised me to take the banking exams as soon as possible so that I could benefit from the practise I had had at school. (All the other staff members were unqualified and he encouraged me to be not like them) There were five compulsory subjects and there were two parts to each. You had to pass the first part before taking the second. So I said I would take all five at one go and joined the Metropolitan College (by

12

correspondence) which my father had used for his Insurance studies. He had finished up as a marker of students exam papers – no doubt for some small fee.

I started the studies in November and the exams were set for April. So I had a shorter time than usual to learn and failed the Practise and Law of Banking and also in Commercial English (for which I had done no study at all thinking that it would be well within my school curriculum). This setback made me try very hard and as a reward I passed my finals with Honours and fairly high up the published lists. The pass results had been directed to a post restante in Southern Ireland where I knew I would be on holiday. It was 1934 and I had taken my younger brother, bicycles and tent gear for a two-week holiday.

I had read all about Ireland in H V Morton's book 'In search of Ireland'. It was easy and cheap. I set off with the great sum of £8 and Lol had 30 shillings. Having arrived in Dublin we set off south for the Powers Court Demesne; camped nearby and the following day set off for Killarney. When on this sort of travelling and self-catering we found it very convenient to have a stock of bananas. So every village we passed through we would look for fruit shops but found none that had bananas for sale. Then on a lonely crossroads we saw a group of young people and an accordionist who stopped us and asked if we could dance. This group were involved in making a film and were having a short break. We accepted and were dancing on a concrete square when suddenly they stopped, packed their things and ran off. The cause was the sight of a priest's black hat visible over the wall of a neighbouring field. Very Strange Religion!

We then entered the outskirts of Killarney and spotted a fruit shop. I told the shopkeeper of our attempts to find bananas in all previous villages. He asked me if we had been through a particular one and I said 'Yes'. To which he said well that was my brother's shop. If you had only known you could have told him that you had met me!! Naturally we visited Blarney Castle and obviously had to kiss the Blarney Stone which makes you lucky for the rest of your life and gives you 'the gift of the gab'. After five days and nights at a Killarney local farm I asked the farmer's wife how much I owed her. She listed the items we had had, eggs, milk, bread etc. and said that will be two shillings please. So I gave her an extra sixpence for her children and she seemed delighted. Their granddad had asked me if we could buy guns, (rifles) in UK and could we bring him one next time, and when I asked him what he wanted to shoot, he said 'Men, of course', by which time he was hitting the ground with his walking stick.

After a shortish period in Chesterfield, I was moved to a small branch in Sheffield. It was in Pinstone Street and it had a staff of only three. The manager was a Mr Palfreyman Walker and he had many strange habits, all designed to save money and make a profit for the bank. He did not allow us to have the heating on until it was really freezing and would make us go down into the basement to get warm through swinging a golf club on the cement floor. I got so good that I could hit a match stick that was laid flat without hitting the cement! The other member of staff was George Seabrook whose father was the manager of the major branch in Harrogate. He was a very able clerk/cashier with an attractive personality. He could play the piano very well, liked women and whisky.

On one occasion when we were running the branch without the manager in winter conditions, I had been stoking up the gas fired boiler and had been in the cellar making coffee etc. Towards the end of the afternoon I began to feel woozy, light headed and pulse fairly fast. As I shut the outer door at three o'clock and turned to come back into the office I keeled over and lost consciousness. George came to my rescue and opened the front door to let the fresh air blow over me – he had realised what the trouble was – carbon monoxide from the gas boiler; also dashed down and turned off the gas heater. If it had not been for him I could very well have died.

My next move was to a much busier branch at the bottom of the Moor and the junctions of London Road, Cemetery Road and Ecclesall Road. This branch had living quarters above the office and this was occupied by the manager 'Daddy' Williams. His chief clerk/cashier was a Mr Aubrey. My immediate senior was a Derek Wilde who was 6ft 5inches tall, very bright and with an attractive personality. He had taken his bank exams and had then taken a law degree. He ended up as the Chief General Manager of the bank before transferring to Kleinwort Benson, Merchant Bankers for the last years of his service.

When the manager went on holiday it was the rule that the living accommodation had to be occupied by a member of the staff. You have guessed it. It was to be my privilege. So they had to provide me with breakfast (I specified all the luxuries I could think of) and they boarded out the normally live in 'maid'. There were some amusing incidents during these holiday spells. Once when I opened the back door to let the maid in, I saw that the whole building was circled by fire

15

hoses and fire engines were also on all sides. There had been a serious fire in a nearby factory and I had slept through it all.

On another occasion I had come back to occupy the Bank House at about midnight and decided to practise my Tap Dancing on the parquet flooring which was on the customers side of the counter. At about two in the morning the back door was being loudly hammered. It woke me up and when I got down to answer it I found two burly policemen. They told me it had been reported that a hammer and chisel had been heard by passers-by, being used in the bank. I let them in and showed them that all was well but I did not tell them the real cause. It was put down as a false report to waste police time!

Another amusing incident occurred when we had trouble with the strong room door. It was sited in the Managers room and was locked by three very long keys. For some reason it would not open and the days work could not start. All the ledgers, cash and other records were all stored in this strong room. So they telephoned for emergency help from the safe makers (I think they were called Milners). The locksmith arrived and promptly asked the Manager to leave the room as he would not work while he was in the room. Somewhat disgruntled, Mr Williams came out and shut the door behind him. He had no sooner reached where we were all standing than the door was opened by the expert and the safe door was open. **We had not been allowed to see how it was so easily done!**
I remember that this office was on the inner junction of Cemetery Road and London Road, and our building formed a rounded point overlooking the junction with a view right up the central main road called The Moor. There was a point

duty policeman directing traffic at this junction (it is now a huge roundabout) and one officer in particular was very impressionable and funny to watch. There was a small shop on the beginning of Ecclesall Road and they painted sales items on their windows to attract custom. This was painted by an attractive young lady who had to use a step-ladder to reach the top of the glass. She had very attractive legs and when this policeman saw this sight his arms began to wave in all directions and traffic almost came to a halt.

After a few years in the Moor branch I was transferred to the Main branch in the centre of Sheffield. It was called Fitzalan Square Branch and had the main commercial accounts of the big industrial companies of Sheffield. The staff there consisted of a Manager, Chief Clerk, four or five cashiers (Billy Hind was the chief cashier), four or five ledger clerks, several juniors and pass book clerks, securities clerk, and two uniformed messengers.

The Manager was a Mr Chamberlain. The chief clerk was a Mr Dyson and the manager's secretary was a Miss Winnie Webster. At that time the senior staff included Frank Swindells (who later became manager of Doncaster branch after the war), Tommy Gibbins (who became manager of Worksop branch after the war) and Harry Manning who had come from chief foreign branch where Elsie and Doris Waters (Comediennes) had once worked, and Sam Howarth. It was this same Sam Howarth who after the war and under a different manager, George Briggs was being told off for some minor incompetence. Briggs harangued him for about 15 minutes – the door was ajar and the other staff could hear the tirade – when Sam came out he left the manager frothing at the mouth. Sam announced to all his colleagues "I don't think he likes me" and the door was still open so the manager must have heard the comment!

There was a girl clerk called Barbara Somerfield who was a member of the Croft House Operatic Society which produced musical operettas once a year. They were put on at any one of the main theatres in Sheffield for a whole week. There was music and dancing, and as I could tap dance and had had voice production lessons from a Belle Canto teacher called Moseley I duly joined in and was accepted for the chorus and dance troupe. This entailed about six months of hard work until the day of the big opening night. We had a great deal of fun and were generally reckoned to be at professional standard.

Another activity was organised by our local Director, 'Freddy' Seebohm, later to be knighted, and this was at the Sheffield University where we used their gymnasium and had fitness workouts. One exercise was to see how far we could throw the heavy medicine ball along a row of 3 mattresses. Most could only achieve ½ way. When it was my turn I put all my effort into a scientific style and threw the weight past the end of the third mattress! It was here that I broke my front teeth. I had dived to collect the heavy medicine ball which I thought was going to pass through the legs of another player. However he jumped backwards, bottom first in order to catch it. I unfortunately bit his bottom and that was the start of tooth problems, a partial plate and then finally full dentures in the early 1950's.

I met and palled up with a Bill Rees who boarded nearby. He was a surveyor/valuer for the Corporation and through his interest I began to do rock climbing and mountaineering, the latter with Bill's friend (also Welsh), who was also a valuer and was so good a climber that he finally climbed Everest.

I also played golf after lessons from Willie Wallis at the Hallamshire Golf Club. I played tennis at the Bamford Tennis Club and made a circle of friends there in the Hope Valley and swam at the pool at the Rising Sun Hotel near Bamford and rambled of course.

At this time my brother, Laurence (Lol) had finished school at the De La Salle College (my father had to pay for this school as Lol had not passed his 11 plus). So my father took him into his office The Friends Provident Insurance. Here he tried to take the Preliminary Insurance Exams to qualify for the full qualifications. There were only three subjects and he failed in one different subject on three attempts. It was while working here that a Spiritual Medium told him about his spiritual age and that he would not do well in this type of job and would do best of all in Australia or New Zealand. So he resigned from his job as being unsuited to his abilities. Instead he joined the RAF where he could do very well all the mechanical tests whether on engines or on the wings and fuselage, thus fulfilling the prognosis of the phrenologist O'Neil when Lol was only six.

O'Neil was an umbrella man who had called at our house when Lol was about six: felt his head bumps and pronounced that he would be able to do anything with his hands – but not be academic. At that age he could dismantle a watch, including the extraction of the coil spring from its special container, and re-assemble it with perfect result.

It was at this office that I once met my father's Head Office Actuary. When my father told him I was good at figures he asked me to write down ten large sums of money (in pounds, shillings and pence) in order to show that I could add up accurately. So I did this starting in the tens of thousands. He just looked at the list and wrote down an answer starting at the pounds. When I had finished my addition he showed me his answer, it was the same as mine. Then he asked me to do a multiplication of five digits by five digits. Again he looked at my figures and wrote down the answer. My eventual answer agreed with his. He must have had a personal calculator. So I don't think he was particularly impressed by my efforts even though I was accurate.

Shortly before the end of 1937 the branch was mechanised. There had to be a squad of operators and they chose us young ones rather than the old hand-writing clerks. I was one of the pupils. The machines were called Mercedes and were powered by electric drive, we were trained to operate the various keyboards and combined typewriter by touch. We could do about 350 to 500 entries an hour. The glamorous instructress could do 800.

Shortly after that we were getting warning of the likelihood of war and I joined the TA Cavalry, Yorkshire Dragoons 'A' Squadron which was based in Sheffield.

My Life in the Army

During 1937 and more so in 1938 it was becoming ever more obvious that England was going to go to war with Germany. There were all kind of preparations being made both officially and privately. The possibility of air raids was the start of A.R.P. and my father became very interested. So much so that eventually he was appointed Officer in Charge of the Southern Division A.R.P. for Sheffield.

It became a common topic of conversation, among my contemporaries, and in general. What are you going to do in the coming war? What arm of the Army, Navy or Air Force are you going to join? I felt that it would be best to make the choice myself and thereby get into an organisation that would be of interest, rather than compelled to join a unit without an option.

So I joined the Territorial Army; 'A' Squadron, The Yorkshire Dragoons. They were stationed in Sheffield with a headquarters in Doncaster and they were still 'horsed'. I had always had a wish to ride. This way I would be taught properly and without the option.

The formalities were quickly completed and we were quickly introduced to our non- commissioned officers. S.M. Eric Roberts was in charge, I liked him and his dry sense of humour, gruff though it often seemed. We started riding school, at a covered 'school' in Gell Street, off West Street, Sheffield. We also had various 'week-ends' of training and doing exercises with horses – one such was at Hassop Hall, the then home of our Colonel, Sir Francis Stephenson. There

21

was a lot of very hard work; cleaning tack and stables; grooming your horse; feeding and watering and I just loved it; and the camaraderie. This went on throughout 1938 and 1939. In the early part of 1939 we actually went to a camp for two weeks. It was held on the banks of the South Tyne River, in a lovely estate. That was an exciting period, for which I had a free extra holiday from the bank, and I think we were paid a wage of about 10/-. Once at Gell Street riding school we were doing passive riding over jumps. This entailed tying the reins behind the horse's neck, crossing your arms, and following the instructions of the Sergeant Major over a series of low jumps. I was the last of the trainees to fall off, whereupon the S. M. said 'Got you, you b.... Who told you to dismount?

Then in the last few days of August **WAR** was declared and the T.A. was mobilised on the 27/29 August and we were all called up.

In a very short time we assembled in a camp near Malton, Yorkshire with all the other squadrons of the regiment. Eventually we were all equipped with khaki uniforms and a few weeks later collected our requisitioned horses from Malton railway station. We rode them back to our camp, riding one and leading three others; it was very exciting and also quite demanding on strength and ability.

Having received our supply of horses, which I believe were requisitioned at the low price of £40.00 each from hunting sources, they were all sorted out to each squadron by the Sgt/Ms. They took the best for themselves and the officers of course and because Sgt. Matt Sheppard was a friend he helped me to get a light boned mare that had come with a special ticket from its 'lady' owner. It was a very good horse, well schooled, and a very good jumper. It had the habit of what I called 'cat' jumping. From very close to the jump it would go up very vertically and equally come down very steeply. This had the effect of loosening me from my saddle – to the great amusement of all who saw it. The fall would also cost me a drink for all who saw it happen. I must have come off a dozen times before I learned to grip extra tightly on the descent.

We were also made to make horse lines for tethering the horses when in open country. We had a wonderful time knocking 6" nails into planks of wood etc. and there were lots of these nailed planks lying around until required. I stepped on one of these while wearing rubber Wellington boots. The nail came right through and came out above the rubber. I had to report to the M.O. who gave me an anti-tetanus jab, an aspirin and back to duty.

Another more serious accident happened in another squadron. The troopers were being directed by their Sgt/M to ride the newly saddled hunters that they had been donated. One was a magnificent animal, possibly a stallion, a 'rig', full of energy and strength which started bucking as soon as the novice got into the saddle. They all came off in quick time. The S/M was advising them how to deal with this difficult horse which was obviously suffering from 'cold back', (or the effect of not having had a saddle on for the non hunting season). Anyway one of his squad said 'I bet you could ride him Sergeant Major' and he could not refuse the challenge. He therefore got the stirrups lengthened to his size, mounted the horse, and it promptly started to react. Finally it bucked viciously and the *surcingle* broke, the rider still gripping the saddle between his knees, and he went up into the air and slightly to the rear of the horse. At this point the horse put his head down, watched the rider's position, and lashed out with both back legs. The unfortunate rider was slowly turning forward as he fell and the hooves hit him on the head and he was dead before he hit the ground. The novice troopers were shocked, and the horse was shot.

After some time we were moved by railway to a new camp near Louth, centred on a beautiful hall which was commandeered and in which we lived etc. It was called Girsby Manor and it had panelled rooms which were so precious that we had to promise not to knock any nails into the wood work for such as hanging clothes or equipment on them. And we never did as far as our lot were concerned. But the amateurish constructions we erected to support our stuff looked a very messy sight and would sometimes collapse over the sleeping bodies that had disturbed their delicate balance. (I can still hear the swear words and calls for help from under the piles of clothing and rifles and equipment).

It was on our way down to Louth that we were routed through York station. We stopped there for water etc. and were allowed off the train for a break. Quite by chance I met a bank colleague, Ken Muxlow, - a few years my senior in the bank. He was being transferred to an active war area. He was subsequently injured in north Italy and suffered a bullet through the face which entered at one side and came out the other. He had been on reccy and was watching tracer bullets passing fairly close to his position when it happened; he put his head a little too far forward in his eagerness to pinpoint the source of the fire. He survived the injury but had the lasting effect of not being able to activate the muscles of one side of his face. He was a very fine athlete and an efficient bank clerk. We once won the three-legged race; (he more or less carried me), and the wheel-barrow race at the Bankers Sports, held just before the war on the Abbeydale Sports Ground. His father and his sister also worked in the bank. After the war, I joined Dorothy Muxlow, his sister, at Local Head Office when I was promoted to be the LHO Chief Clerk in 1954, and Dorothy was the very efficient secretary to the District Manager (Tom Speet).

Another funny incident happened while at York station. One of our young officers, Peter Smith, got out of the train to get a tray of coffee and drinks for his party and the train started and left the platform just as he was returning. He was not fazed – turned about and got into a taxi and directed it to travel as fast as possible to the station in Doncaster, where he knew the train was to have a further stop. When we got to Doncaster we all cheered as he walked nonchalantly onto the platform, tray of drinks still in his hands.

Many funny things happened while at Girsby Manor. Some of the lads were guilty of some 'high jinks' while slightly inebriated which resulted in some of the farm chickens meeting an early death. As punishment they were put on 'jankers' in their case what we came to call 'sludge bumping', wheel-barrowing away gallons and gallons of mud from the drives in the farm areas used by the army. And that effort was after full normal duties. The leg-pulling and witty remarks were perhaps the hardest part of their punishment. Another occasion concerned the fetching of a special supply of beer from Grimsby for a celebration. The lads who fetched it, in one of the private cars owned by one of them, came back the worse for drink; they had consumed all the bottled stock and there was only one barrel left!

We were visited by lots of friends and relatives as it was known that we would soon be departing overseas. One such was Capt. Matt Sheppard who had earned his commission in the 1st Great War, also in the Yorkshire Dragoons. His son Sgt Matt was our Sgt and a wonderful man he was; always cheerful and helpful, always.

As part of efforts to build morale the regiment was invited to join the local hunt, and that was very exciting. We also had instruction in charging with sabres drawn. On one such occasion, George Beal, the squadron clerk, who because of that position missed a lot of riding practise; was ordered to take part in a 'Generals Inspection' 'mock' parade and charge. It was raining hard and we were all wearing tin hats, waterproof capes and full gear. On the command being given to draw swords and charge, line after line of closely ridden horses charged from one end of the 25 acre field to the other which ended in a high hawthorn hedge. George's horse would not heed George's command to stop and only the hedge stopped him – George did not stop on the horse but flew gaily on over the hedge. He came out rather unsteadily, miraculously unhurt, cheered by all of his friends.

It was at this time that all inoculations had to be completed. Our Squadron leader, a Major Eustace Stephenson, brother of the Commanding Officer, and called by the ranks Useless Eustace, headed the queue for the JABS. Knowing that he would almost certainly faint at being 'pricked' he had a chair placed strategically close and duly fainted. We were all very much encouraged! I can remember having my course of jabs. Normally we were given a 24 hour off duty – some even took the time to make a quick trip to see loved ones – having no car I spent my time off in camp sweating it out in bed. The duty corporal, Cosgrove, asked if I would like a mug of tea and he brought me a 'real Sgt Major's mug'. The spoon would stand up in the tea leaves after I had drunk the contents!! It certainly stimulated me back to near normal.

The next big event was to plan for the transport of the horses to the Middle East. A selection was made to have the horse party made up of the most experienced resourceful troopers. They would be on a different ship from the main party. I was to have been on this draft, but was sent on an Officer Selection Board for an immediate commission. This was held in Newark and took all of two days. I was judged not to have sufficient experience and was returned to unit. And that meant that I was a mere passenger on the troopship and travelled through France by train in comparative comfort (8 to each compartment and 2 days journey time to Marseille). We heard later that the horse party had discovered that their horse count before embarking the next day was short of 15 horses. The SM detailed a party to go out into the horse lines and 'win' enough to make up the shortfall. They did this and ended up with a useful surplus!

The sail through the Mediterranean was uneventful and very interesting. Seeing flying fish phosphorescence etc. and we landed in HAIFA towards the end of December 1939.

In the next few months we made and used various camps south of Haifa. We occupied large marquee size tents with a double roof, in various places. Karkur, Latrun and Kahl Mansura come to mind and training went on all the time. It was when we got to Mansura – at the foot of the Mount of Sacrifice that things began to develop for me. (See also item under "Dreams").

Firstly George Beal was taken to Head Quarters Squadron of the Regiment as secretary or (Orderly Room Sgt as he was known). We therefore, were without his expert administration and I was co-opted to replace him for the Squadron.

It may interest you to hear that George Beal had a very surprising ability. He could remember the army number of every one of 'A' squadron. These numbers consisted of 7 or 8 digits and we would while away the time, when permitted, to test his memory. 'What's my number George?' would ring out and George would oblige – he was never wrong. When he took on the additional numbers of the full regiment he could do the same for the whole lot within about three months through typing out army orders.

At about this time the Battle of Britain was raging. We would hear the radio news of the devastation being caused by the German bombing and it deeply affected the morale of the men. I tried to counter this effect by listening to the news of our fighter successes, and would type out the daily score. German bombers shot down 130 or whatever as against single figure losses. The men felt they would rather have been at home defending their wives and loved ones. The Army Command in Cairo acknowledged the problem, which was very widely spread, by supplying every unit with radio sets and loud speakers to receive a special message broadcast (and to be listened to as an order) by General Wavell, Cairo H.Q.

Shortly after I had taken over from George Beal I had to help the Orderly Officer to pay the men. After we had completed the pay-out I made a summary of the sum paid out, deducted it from the starting fund, and said the remainder should be so much, and I'm pleased to say that that is the sum that I have here to hand over.

The Orderly Officer said 'Good God, that's the first time I have balanced the books since the start of the war'! Then the bombshell fell. Brigade Head Quarters at Sarafand sent in an order to Sergeant Major Roberts telling him to send a clerk for extra regimental duty on a permanent basis to Brigade Head Quarters. S/M Roberts returned signal to say we did not have one, with an anxious wink at me. It did not work, for by return came a new order which read 'Send Trooper A.S.Bellinger – he's a bank clerk'. So that was the start of an unexpected, major change – leaving all my pals, and the horses, and very good they were, and moving into unknown territory.

IT PROBABLY SAVED MY LIFE.

While at the foot of the Mount of Sacrifice, I had climbed the mountain 4 or 5 times and met the monks etc. They eventually told me that I would not be seeing them anymore and would like me to have a memento of my visits – the choice of two oak walking sticks. I chose the smaller one as it would go into my kit bag – and I still have it. Within days Brigade Head Quarters had me transferred from the Yorkshire Dragoons.

For the Yorkshire Dragoons were mechanised and went through the El Allamien Desert campaign, Italy Anzio Beach Head, and faced many casualties before getting back to Sheffield in September 1944. My troop suffered 16 deaths and many wounded; only four were unscathed and I was one of the four.

During the early months of my time in Palestine (December 1939 and into January to March 1940) I began to experience some difficulty in controlling my bladder. I think this was probably caused by the very great differences in the day and night temperatures, it could reach the high 90's during the day and it was almost freezing cold in the early hours of the night. When going to bed it was too hot to use a blanket and when asleep it would drop in temperature by as much as 60 – 70 degrees Fahrenheit. This gave me a chill on the abdomen, bladder etc. and I was 'caught short' while on parade on several occasions. This resulted in being charged 'with disorderly conduct' to put it politely and to protect myself I had to report 'sick'.

The MO was very understanding and decided that it should be properly investigated by the local army general hospital which was in or near Haifa. So I duly attended as an IN patient and started being assessed. This resulted eventually in my being given a cystoscopy examination, without any form of anaesthetic, and this was quite uncomfortable to say the least. The final result was that they decided I had a congenitally small bladder – I was not malingering; and it would therefore be necessary to change my health category from A1 to B9. They interviewed me and said that if I wished I could be discharged from the army on grounds of health. I said that I did not wish to leave the army and would prefer to accept the lowered category and find a niche in the services that was suitable. So that is what they agreed to do and my new health rating of B9 was duly carried out and I went back to my unit where it made no difference at all!!!!

While in this hospital, I think it was number 23 general, there were some very interesting incidents. There were some 24 beds in my ward which dealt with surgical cases and the man in the next bed to me had an investigatory operation. He came back from theatre with a large square of Elastoplast over the region of his diaphragm. When the surgeon came on his rounds next day he looked at this man and said that he needed to remove the dressing to inspect the wound. He started to get a corner of the plaster free and then said 'I will leave you to get it all off while I go round the rest of the patients'. So this lad worked at it, wincing at the pain caused by the sticky resistance. When the doctor finally came back the lad had just got enough to give the doctor a good grip. He took hold of the corner and said 'You don't appear to have made much progress do you? Would you like a little more time to get it off? To which the lad said 'Oh yes please sir. I would like that as it hurts so much as I pull it'. At this point without any further warning the doctor gave the Elastoplast a great heave and took it completely clear in one last effort. The soldier squealed his shocked response, rose about two feet 'horizontally' before sinking back very relieved on to his back.

Another case involved an Australian soldier who had come into hospital with acute appendicitis. Also in the ward was another Australian who had the peace time job of Life Guard on Bondi Beach, near Sydney. Apparently he had had this same operation while in his civilian job. He had had the very best surgeon to carry out his operation with the main aim of having as small a scar as possible. His surgeon had pinpointed the exact location of the appendix by getting a 'ball' of wool to pass over his operation area and noting the pain reaction., the scar for this old operation was only a mere 1½ inches.

When the lad came back from theatre, his scar was examined by all members of the ward, to their great amusement the scar showed that the surgeon had obviously been looking for the appendix and had made a zigzag of three four inch joined cuts. All the observers gave their approval with laughter and 'cheers mate'.

Another humorous lad was obviously a Yorkshire miner. He was quite small and would sing funny songs, one in particular concerned all different parts of the skeleton (knee knocker this leg bones, thigh bones etc). He also conducted a fantasy game of dice. He pretended to be one of several players and would imitate the rattle of the dice in the box by shaking his head vigorously from side to side and allowing his dentures to knock against each other, with his mouth partly open so that the sound could be heard by the other occupants of the ward. After about a week in this process I was sent for two weeks to a rehabilitation camp at Hadera on the coast. And it was here that I experienced the events which inspired the title for my book mentioned in the introduction, 'Voices from the dark'.

My barrack hut contained about 30 beds – all occupied by sick and wounded soldiers who were all there for as long as it took to get fit enough to return to their units.

I was most interested in the man who was next to me. He was a Yemenite Arab who had broken his leg. This was now in a full length pot or plaster. 'Lights out' was at 9.15 p.m. and by then it was completely dark. As soon as this happened the Yemenite would call out "Johnny you teach me new word." The response was quite remarkable – voices from the other beds would call out a word – he would copy it and so on for as long as an hour or even more.

Having got a new word, the Yemenite would string a few together, and the voices from the dark would correct his sentences if necessary. By the end of my stay there he could carry on quite a good conversation and make himself understood in English. I remember he was not very tall but he was very strong. He could stand beside his single bed and swing his bad leg up and jump sideways clean over his bed.

Recounting this story to my granddaughter Chalene and our friend Claire Selfridge they both said **"Voices from the Dark!"** that would make a very good title for your book." So I hereby make acknowledgement to them for the gift suggestion.

SARAFAND was the name of a huge camp where the Brigade Headquarters were sited. It was composed of a great many wooden hutted buildings where formerly men and army families had been accommodated. The families had all been moved recently to South Africa for safety, making all the buildings available for other use; there were all kinds of special training courses; a hospital; and we were to form a huge transit camp. This latter was to house soldiers while on courses; and whole units on the move from one theatre of war to another; and finally to accommodate special units for temporary stays while doing such things as map making for the Syrian/Lebanese campaigns, etc.

It was my duty to set up the administration and become the Orderly Sergeant or Chief Clerk. After a short time under a temporary C. O. he left and was replaced by a Major Hugh McTavish of the Black Watch. He had been President of Military Courts and had a great deal to do with the pre-war administration of Palestine. There had been quite a number of terrorist type attacks against the regime and oil pipe lines and similar installations were the subject of bombings, military vehicles were often targeted and were frequently damaged by land mines and similar devices. He would try these 'villains' and if found guilty he would condemn them to death. He said that these culprits were hanged, rather than shot and he would attend each execution as the officer in charge.

When I had become fully established in the Transit Camp I wrote to my mother and let her know I was enjoying the comfort of a proper bed and also the luxury of sheets in my bed. Eventually I received her reply in which she said she was glad I was so comfortable – but would I not be safer in the Navy – you can swim can't you?

McTavish had genuine respect for the Arab culprits – they had no fear of death – and would thank him a thousand times for his 'kindness' as they walked passed him (shackled at the ankles and wrists, with their hands behind their backs, by steel chains), on their way to the 'drop' platform. After they had dropped, he would inspect and 'spin' the hanging body to check that death had taken place. He certainly was a very phlegmatic character. Another illustration of this respect for the Arabs' lack of fear for death occurred one day in Jaffa at the bank where we had gone to collect money to pay our staff. It was at the Barclays Bank D C & O where the car park was under the banking area. While I counted the money, that we had drawn, Major McTavish had been provided with coffee. Then as we left the car park area we were approached by a young Arab boy – of possibly 7 or 8 years of age. The side window was fully wound down and the boy's head came just above the opening. He asked for 'baksheesh' and Mc said to me 'Just watch this' With that he picked up his colt automatic pistol with his left hand and held the weapon up to the face of the boy and said "I'm going to shoot you, you little bastard". The boy actually laughed and said 'Go on Sir, pull the trigger'. Within a few yards as we were about to join the actual road we were again approached, in a similar way to that of the boy, but this time by a very large young Jewish man. Again Mc said 'Watch this' and he repeated his action with the pistol. The effect on the big strong looking young man was dramatic. He went pale and almost collapsed. McTavish was highly delighted with the success of his demonstration. It had been very convincing and it had put my C O into a very happy mood. Major McTavish had been hit by shrapnel in his right wrist during the First World War and the hand had been reset off centre about ¾ inch towards the thumb. The shrapnel had hit his two watches (kept for synchronising time on ops.) and the metal had gone through the wrist and into his thigh. But he could hit a crown piece at twenty paces without taking aim – an instinctive aim method of just pointing!!

The transit camp was formed out of many wooden barrack huts in its own area. Each hut would have accommodation for, say, 30 beds with toilet facilities at each end. All had electric lighting and iron, free standing stoves to provide heat in the colder months.

Our Sergeant Major was called Bob Blohm of the Sherwood Foresters and he had been recruited from his battalion that was based in Cyprus. He was a tall and very strong man who looked not unlike Clark Gable; he had been training Cypriot men recruits. He said they were so weak, constitutionally, that they had to have rest periods every twenty minutes! The incidence of insipient V.D. was very high indeed – in fact the War Diary which I used to receive had the % incidence above 98%. He smoked the free ration of cigarettes at the rate of about 100 per day. Every morning the first 'drag' would cause him to cough for at least 15 minutes, after which he would take a deep breath and say 'That's better'. The 'Staff' N. C. O.s were S.M; S. Sergeant; Quartermaster Sgt. Percy Blow, Sergeant Dave Boyle (of the Cheshire Yeomanry) and 'me' Sergeant in charge of administration. We were the core that ran the ship and we were within 100 yards of Brigade Headquarters. At bedtime we had separate bedrooms in a 4 apartment hut which had the extra comfort of a small veranda. Each room had an electric fan in the ceiling and hooks from which to suspend our sand fly nets. The beds were cast iron which folded into half size and the mattresses were made up of three 'Biscuits'. When I decided to de–bug the seams, I found that Bob Blohm's were lined by hundreds of the nasty blood-sucking creatures – though he said he had never had any and certainly never felt the pain of their activities. (He was always a very heavy sleeper due to influence of a few bedtime drinks!). The first time he and I paid out the troops we finished up with a great many 'a quittance rolls' (one for each different regiment). After the last soldier had left the parade, Blohm gave me half the pile of pay sheets and asked me to 'cast them'. This I did, at my desk, in about five minutes. I took them back to him and stood diffidently at his side. He was still working on the first of his pile – looked up at me and said 'When I said "cast them" I meant you had to add them up'. I replied that that is what I thought he meant and that I had done just that. He said 'Good God – take mine'. He could not believe that I could have done this simple task so quickly. But he was a very knowledgeable army man and an ex Olympic swordsman I believe; and a hell of a man with the girls.

In the early days with many different soldiers on courses or in transit between war zones we had some problems with pilfering in the B/Huts. When Major McTavish was told he called them all together on a special parade. He said he would not put up with this behaviour; he appointed two guards to each hut with permission to attend late for breakfast to give time for camp guards to take over. And then he said that if the culprits were found and were brought to him with their fingers, arms and legs broken; he would still give them the maximum prison sentences. The pilfering stopped like magic!

The move to Sarafand with its increased responsibilities for me resulted eventually in promotion. I was promoted to acting Sergeant with the appropriate rise in pay and standing. For example I could now enter the holy of holies, the 'Sergeants Mess'. Major McTavish admitted to me that he knew nothing about money or accounting for it and put himself 'in my capable hands' as he put it. He was also very generous and thoughtful where we staff were concerned and had a great sense of humour. One of his abilities was to be able to speak a few typical sentences in many different dialects. So this enabled him to speak a little topical slang or dialect to the men wherever they came from in the U.K. The men liked that very much and became a very willing team.

When he came out to Palestine before the war he had brought with him his own private motor car, it was a very fine Ford Lincoln Zephyr. He got high octane petrol from friendly RAF officers from Lydda air base (now an airport) and this made the car fly along. We went on a few trips together. One such was to journey to Acre and en route we called at a lovely little bay which had been a centre for the early Crusaders, with ruined castle type buildings just ashore. I was able to have a swim here while McTavish had a smoke and a short rest. The historic place was called Athlit Caesarea. The place had been taken over by a chatty pot maker, red clay water carrying pots which being slightly porous would allow the contents to pass through to the surface where the heat caused a rapid evaporation, which in turn caused the contents to reduce in temperature. Very effective water coolers!

Another of McTavish's kindnesses was his special authorisation to permit me to carry a camera and take photographs without hindrance. I got many interesting shots of dive bombers over Haifa; shots of VIP's such as Anthony Eden and General Wavell. The latter at close range when he came to see McTavish immediately prior to going to UK for urgent talks with Churchill and the War Council at about the time when the Allies were driven out of Greece etc. He had found the time to stop off in Lydda to pick up a letter from McTavish to his wife with the promise that he would be back within about three days with the reply. At that time, the normal time scale was about six weeks – the Mediterranean having been barred after Italy came into the war. All mail then had to come via South Africa and this had a very morale affecting pressure on all ranks.

The camera I had been able to buy came from escapees from Nazi occupied countries who had come out with whatever they could carry easily from Germany and I bought two cameras of great quality in this way. One was a Leica and the other a Zeiss both were 35mm with wonderful lenses and I was delighted to be able to go round all the Holy places on short periods of leave, taking memorable shots throughout. As a matter of interest when I got back to civilian life I was able to sell these cameras for a lot more than I had paid for them – particularly helpful when I was trying to buy furniture to set up home for the first time since getting married in 1942.

One of the interesting things that has occurred since the war was the chance to read the book by the Countess of Ranfurly, Hermione, in which she tells a very interesting story of how she followed her future husband into the Middle Eastern war and became involved, as a civilian, at G H Q Cairo. She mentions in the book that at about the time that General Wavell was transferred to the Indian War Area, they had somehow acquired a very good civilian car called a Ford Lincoln Zephyr. I can tell you where it came from. It had been the car that my Transit Camp C O had brought out from England just before the war started when he had been appointed the 'President of Military Courts'.

When he heard his great friend Wavell was to transfer to the Indian theatre, he accepted Wavell's invitation to go with him to set up a similar Transit Camp such as ours. The car would then have been taken to Cairo for the use of H Q 'High ups'.

I only read the book a short time before seeing the obituary of Hermione, Countess of Ranfurly which appeared in the Telegraph of Tuesday 13th February 2001. She had died aged 87 years and her husband had predeceased her in 1988, after which she had concentrated on her diaries. She kept horses and two fat Spaniels and many pictures. She also chain smoked into her eighties, quite some character and what a co-incidence. I felt almost as if I should have met her if only I had stayed out in the Middle East Theatre.

As Christmas 1941 approached Major McTavish had said he was more interested in the New Year celebrations than in Christmas and we could all have leaves or time off at Christmas but not at the New Year. He then arranged for a special party with free Beer Tent and loads of food etc for New Years Eve. I have a photograph of the table layout and the huge beer barrel 'supported' by the two head cooks. It was a very good party.

In 1941, at Christmas time, my regiment, the Yorkshire Dragoons were stationed in the Castle in Acre, in the very north of Palestine. My old Regimental friends contacted me and asked if I could possibly get leave to join them for the festivities in their Sergeants Mess. I told them I was still only a corporal at that time. They said that was not a worry; they would bring the additional stripes for my use and nobody would know enough to object or make trouble for me. I readily agreed and I was duly spirited away to Acre.

The main purpose of the invitation was so that the 'A' Squadron Sergeants could use me in the shooting competitions they had planned (did I say that I was the regimental marksman? I was). On the day of Christmas 1941 the competition was duly 'fought', using 'morris–tubed' service Enfield rifles with a bore 22mm and various short ranged competitions which included swinging bottles etc. I duly won first prize and we had a very happy time. Transport then returned me to Sarafand, I can't remember the distance but it was quite a long journey, of long straight roads and lots of dust everywhere.

I was back in good time to complete the arrangement for our own special New Years Party. I remember that in honour of the Scottish Commanding Officer we had a sign erected at the end of the dining room which proclaimed, 'LANG MAY YUR LUM REEK' and the N.C.O.'s and Officers served the other ranks and had their meal after they had seen everyone satisfied.

It was at about this time that McTavish asked me to attend at Brigade H.Q. to see the Major in charge to tell him a story that I had earlier told McTavish. It had to be told in a broad Yorkshire dialect. This I duly did – it was an order – and the Major laughed and returned my salute. He obviously liked

McTavish and could enter into the spirit.

There was a unit of New Zealand specialists who came and occupied a separate hut. They were map makers, and their duty was to provide large scale maps for any particular war area in advance of any action. They had a huge camera mounted on tracks with suitable easels so that focusing of the hand drawn maps could be copied, enlarged and repeated in great numbers. They were a highly intelligent group and they got up to all kinds of high jinks when work was over. One example was in their barrack hut which was provided with beds made out of wicker frames. They went round the room jumping from one to the next in mad races – the results being that the beds were soon wrecked and un-useable; likewise with wicker arm chairs. They sat in these and gripping the arms would 'jump' them in races from one end to the other of the barrack hut. They did not last long either. But they found relief and fun in this activity.

While at the transit camp unit I took a few days off and did the round of the Jerusalem holy places. I also did a trip down to Jericho. I went in a native bus which was occupied entirely by Arab passengers. Once we got going they called out 'Jonny you teach us new words in English'. So this I did and they could all say lots of new words by the time we arrived in Jericho. The journey was also interesting in that the bus would stop at various places – in barren featureless areas and they would either put a passenger down (complete with baggage or sheep and goat) or would pick up a passenger who would appear as though from nowhere. There were never any signs of human habitation. But Jericho was quite different.

In the town centre a friendly Palestine policeman (English) asked me if I would like to be shown round and I readily agreed. The tops of the mountain we could see would be about sea level. There were all kinds of special fruit farms and of course there was the Dead Sea. It was near the end of the year but the heat and sunshine were the equivalent of summer to me. The Palestine Police were a separate body and had been there before the war started and I believe were under the Colonial Office. They were also to be seen in other towns and particularly noticeable in Tel Aviv where we used to go for bathing parades at which I was a 'LIFE GUARD'.

Life at this time was never dull. There were a great many courses to be administered; regiments were being moved via our transit camp; all kinds of battles were being reported in the Western Desert over England; in Greece, Cyprus, Malta and Crete.

In rest periods and short leave passes I often went to bathe in the sea at Tel Aviv, where there was also a friendly 'Soldiers Club' – this was run by very kind ladies of the city. Many were the wives of professionals such as doctors, musicians and business men. Quite a few had been escapees from Germany, Poland or similar countries which had carried out a pogram against the Jewish race in general.

I was very impressed by the way that these ladies had adapted to their new country. They could all speak Hebrew, Arabic, English as well as their native tongues. They could also write these new languages – it made me feel very lazy. One such young woman had come to England, just before the war, from Poland. She had registered at Leeds University for a course in Accountancy and at the time could not speak English. So she went to a language school for the three months prior to her University Course. She got her degree, in English, in the normal time of three years. She could now speak Hebrew, English, Arabic and smatterings of several other languages such as German and Italian. And she was very good looking too. Quite like a particular film star, Jessie Matthews. While in the U K she had met Michael Taylor – a solicitor friend of mine from Sheffield, a fantastic record breaking swimmer who had swum for England in the Commonwealth games and I believe in the Olympics

When Tel Aviv had an Air raid by the Italians there were some Australian troops at the club. When the air raid sirens sounded, all the staff ran into the slit trenches which had been prepared. They had been cut into the sides of the adjoining undeveloped land. Most of the other soldiers followed suit. However, two of the Aussies sneered at the others for their temerity and said that if the bomb had your name on it then that would be that – otherwise 'why hide?' The bombs fell and the two were hit and killed. Their names had been on the weapons!

The route to Tel Aviv from Sarafand passed a glue factory. The glue was made from fish in some special process, and the smell was all pervading. It was very hot and airless, so that we travelled with all windows open, but when we got within a mile or so of this factory we all closed the windows, in an attempt to cut out the smell.

Another interesting bit of social reaction was noticed at the time of special occasions, such as 'Passover' etc. Each of the hostesses would have family parties to which many of us were kindly invited. It was then that each host and hostess had to excuse themselves from their own party just to appear at each of their friends parties to have a drink and say 'how do' etc. If they did not manage to get all round their friends parties there was strong feeling of being 'hurt'. Then they wouldn't speak to each other until the feelings had worn off and forgotten. Quite strange but they all seemed to respond in like manner. We, the guests were very conscious of the feelings it engendered. They seemed to be too sensitive to us.

Tel Aviv was also a centre for Celebrity Concerts and I was lucky enough to attend quite a few of these. I remember that Heifitz, the great violinist was one such and another was the pianist sister of that other wonderful violinist Yehudi Menuhin. On some of these occasions it was possible for us to have all night passes, and we would then stay at some central hotel, to return refreshed on the following morning. It happened on one of these nights; I had gone alone and stayed at this hotel. In the night there was an air raid. The alarm sounded and all the residents had to leave their rooms and go to the shelters – out of the hotel and underground. After the all clear had sounded we all made our way back to our bedrooms. I was sharing a twin bedded room with an unknown service man and he was very slow returning. So I put my money in my trouser pocket, rolled them up and put them under my pillow. I then went off to sleep very heavily. In the morning my trousers were by the door and all the money had gone. It was the same all over the hotel. Apparently an Australian soldier had taken advantage of the situation and had cleaned out all available 'easy' targets. At that time there were about 800 Aussies A.W.O.L. at any one time. They were working in bars, cafes and avoiding capture and service for as long as they could. So I had to ring Dave Boyle and ask him to bring out some rescue cash so that I could pay my hotel bill. It was a very unpleasant experience. But that was typical of the Australian troops. I only met one I would call a gentleman and in contrast I never met a New Zealander who wasn't.

Staying in Tel Aviv one night after attending one of the Celebrity Concerts Dave Boyle, Percy Blow and I made our way out of the hotel through empty streets. We passed a cart which was parked at the side of the road, and it was full of ripe oranges. The oranges had been allowed to ripen on the tree were huge by our standards and very full of juice. One orange would more than fill a ½ pint glass. Anyway, Percy who was a very keen cricketer and bowler decided to show us how good his bowling was. He picked up an orange from the cart and bowled it at a suitable telegraph pole. His aim was deadly accurate and it hit the pole and disintegrated. Percy liked that and sent down quite a few more until we finally had to drag him away, leaving the 'mess' behind us.

On another occasion Boyle and I attended a special party given by the warrant officers of RAF Ramle. Here our friend was a F/Sgt McBain. He was very lively and knew everyone at the RAF camp. One of their stunts to keep us all entertained was to test us for our ability to Fly and Glide. They brought out a strong trestle table and one of their number got onto it face down and clung on strongly by his hands at one end of the table as his companion tipped the table steadily up from the foot end. He finally slid off when the table approached vertical. It was then the turn of one of our lads to accept the challenge and compete to see if he could stay on longer. When he had achieved a suitable angle the RAF lads poured a full glass of cold beer down each trouser leg. Great fun for those who were watching!

In one of our own Sergeants' Mess nights, we had a few N.Z. Maori Sergeants. When asked if they would do something to entertain us, one said he would show us an unusual trick. He took off his shirt and lit a cigarette and asked for the lights to be switched off. He then gripped the unlit end of the cigarette in his navel, and by muscle control made the lighted end glowing in the dark, turn in a circle. Quite remarkable and it duplicated what a member of my old operatic society had demonstrated to chorus members, after the show we had given, before the war. That particular muscle controller had done this for a short time but then had to excuse him-self and dash for the toilets. The movement of his stomach muscles always induced a rapid 'motion'. So try that it you ever suffer from constipation!!

One of the Reservists (they had been called back into service at the start of the war) who was on my deck of the ship carrying us out to Palestine, was called De Athe (or Death). He was very depressed and said that he knew he was not going to survive the war. He was a very experienced horseman as well as being a pleasant personality. Because of these qualities he was chosen by Squadron Leader Major Taylor, to be his batman, stableman, and groom. Major Taylor was then chosen to set up a rehabilitation camp, near Haifa, to help cavalry officers to recover from illnesses etc. It was supplied with a good selection of really good horses and this is where Jerry De Athe came into the scheme. The posting to the Haifa special unit seemed like a passport to safety but something quite unexpected happened.

It was like this. Major Taylor's horse was a very good jumper and Jerry De Athe was schooling it to try to be able to jump a 7 foot gate. He took the horse over a progressively raised gate and then when it got to the 7 foot height it cleared the jump to Jerry's sheer delight. However, the Dhobi Wallahs ((Indian servants who did all the laundry work for the camp) had been using the same gate above which to hang their drying clothes. To do this they had strung a piano wire above the gate from the uprights which also formed the verticals from which the gate was hung. Having dried the clothes they removed them **BUT LEFT THE WIRE** intact. Because there were not any clothes hanging from the wire, the wire was not seen by Jerry; and the wire cut deeply into his throat and he died at the scene.

After the war during my time as manager of the Derby branch I had a customer called Ronnie Marmont. He was at that time Huntsman to the Meynell Hunt and lived at Foston – not far from Derby. Apparently he also had a job at the self same 'Rest Camp' and knew of Jerry De Athe - strange co-incidence. Ronnie was an expert horseman, and maintained livery stables at a grand house where the lady owner had befriended him because he had been very helpful with her horses. Ronnie was very well known in 'horsey circles'; was often a judge at horse shows as well as grooming and training horses as hunters and show horses. I once had a calendar with a picture of Ronnie, mounted on a winning horse, shaking hands with the Queen. He was quite a character. He lived in a flat above the stables which were surrounding a large enclosed square at the rear of this lovely old house. He did all his own washing and one could always see a few pairs of white riding breeches spread out to dry. I knew that he had had to have a new hip (by Darnley the surgeon who developed this operation). He very kindly came and demonstrated its efficiency to a nervous lady customer of mine in Sheffield some years later. He did a full knees bend and a curtsey when I made the introduction. She was convinced and went ahead with her operation the need for which had been an horrific motor accident.

Another of my staff in the camp was a private Jones of the 1st Hamps. He had lost an eye through a workshop accident at Sarafand. There were many very able surgeons in Jerusalem – for the experience they could get in the Middle East where eye problems are very common. They were able to remove the eye without damaging the muscles that move the eye ball. So when they gave him his glass eye it moved almost normally in *cancert* with his real eye. He had been a farm worker in Hampshire before joining the army before the war. He had spent 4 years in the north of India in the foothills of the Himalayas. He weighed about 9 stone, was very fit and had been boxing champion in his unit. He had been a 'scout' with his old unit and could track, etc. and could run up a 7,000 foot hill – he told some wonderful stories about the Ghurkhas with whom they collaborated. These men could shave him without waking him up in a morning as part of their 'batman' duties. By skilful touching they could take the blankets from under a sleeping soldier, without waking him.

He said that on one occasion they got these men to carry the Sergeant Major and his wife, still asleep in their bed, into the middle of the parade ground. (In those times there were married quarters for officers and wives and some families). He didn't tell me what was said when the couple woke up.

They were wonderful trackers and could 'find' for example, buried rifles or similar 'treasure' which had been hidden by forwards troops and carefully concealed, some time ahead of their approach. On two occasions he had been allowed to watch them execute 'Kleftie Wallahs' who had been caught stealing. The sentence was carried out in the same way on each occasion. The guilty man was made to dig his own grave. A double line of Ghurkhas would then form, extending some twenty feet or so from the grave. Then one of the Ghurkhas would be chosen to be the executioner and the prisoner would stand just in front of him facing the grave. He was told that if he could run 'the gauntlet' between the two lines of soldiers and get over the grave – he would be a free man. The executioner would draw his large curved Kukri knife and wait until the exact moment to throw it. On each occasion he had watched the severed head and the body drop separately and neatly into the grave!!! I am sure that he was telling me just as it happened.

Jonesy had another great ability. He could train a wild dog in very quick time to understand his English commands. While demonstrating the tricks he had taught, he also told me that when he had to leave India on the outbreak of war to serve in the Middle East he had taken fond farewell of his batman and had given him a present of 2 rupees. At that time they were worth about 18 to the £1.00 sterling. So I told him how mean I thought he had been after at least two years service. He astonished me when he told me that the two rupees would provide the man with enough to keep him for a whole year. Such was their standard of living!!

As one of my best efforts I was able to take advantage of an army rule and get Jones permission to return to U.K. on compassionate grounds – having been away from his family for over five, nearly six years. He did not know how to thank me and said I must be a parson's son or some such good person. I managed the same for the quartermaster Sergeant Percy Blow. But I never heard anything from them or about them.

Another of my staff, R Carpenter, was later called back to his unit. He had been a bandsman and at one time had the army half mile record in the area he had been in – I think that was India too. He once told me that before each of the official races all contestants had to be passed by the M.O. as fit to compete. They tested his heart and said it was too slow to be safe. He asked to be allowed to run round the track and was then tested again – it was now pumping at a slightly higher rate and he was permitted to run. His normal pulse rate was as low as 40 p.m. and his stride was enormous. He wrote to me after I had got back to U.K. for my commission. He had been wounded in Italy, Monte Cassino, and had lain out all day waiting to be rescued by the RAMC. He survived and got back home to Lancashire. He could no longer run very fast!

Another of my office staff was called Dickie Kirk. He had been a postman in the town of Rotherham (where my future wife lived) and he knew tales about many of their near neighbours! When the Mediterranean Sea was closed and mail became very slow we were allowed one 'telegram' type cable message, outwards per month. He had received a long letter from his wife and was trying to answer this by means of the telegram, and its strict ration of about six words. He was licking his pencil and looking very serious as to how he could achieve his desired effect. I offered to help. He accepted. So I asked him how long he had been married and had he any children etc. He said he had a 16 year old girl and he had been married just before she was born! So I composed the following for him to approve. 'Felicitations reciprocated take care love Dickie'. When he read it he said 'you can't use the word "love"; I've never told her that I love her. I then lectured him to the effect that after all she had done for him he should include the Love word; anyway if he did not love her why had he married her. He said she was the only one of three, who were pregnant by him at the same time, who would not get rid of their baby – so he married her. He said that if he did include the 'love' she would be overjoyed and reply with a letter of at least 16 pages. Her best friend, who was also his mistress, would also send him a long letter of complaint. HE WAS ABSOLUTELY RIGHT. They both wrote as he had predicted!! I think he became a reformed character under my influence.

He also was one of the lucky ones that I managed to get 'Returned to U.K.' under compassionate terms. He took a letter to my Joyce within which was a small very good gold watch with gold bangle 18 ct gold. He got to Rotherham and then posted it so that the delivery would go through 'normal channels'. When Joyce got the envelope the strap was hanging half out of the envelope – but the watch was undamaged and she used it, to the end of her life, on special occasions! It was finally left to one of our granddaughters.

Towards the end of 1941there were changes taking place in the war and it was decided that there would be a change of General to control and conduct the war in the Middle East. General Wavell was to be transferred to the Far East, India etc. And that would be 'of interest' to my C O McTavish his dear friend. Also at this time we received a War Office G H Q Cairo memo regarding the award of various GONGS or military awards. Listed were the medals that were to be awarded. It included the military O.B.E. Mac asked me if I would appreciate the O.B.E. I declined saying that I would prefer to receive my rewards IN HEAVEN. He said that I had done a very good job indeed and that I deserved an award, and this he could guarantee to have approved. Again I said that I had only done my duty using my best effort and banking training etc. and I was happy to have earned his approval. I also said I preferred to get my reward in heaven – seriously. He accepted my decision without further comment. It seemed to me that these awards had come up like the rations and had to be distributed whether deserved or not – a sort of political bit of public relations.

At this time also there was an enquiring message from G.H.Q. as to whether we could make recommendations for certain promotions to commissioned rank. These possibilities were available in several arms of the service. These included the R.A.S.C. and also R.A.P.C. This latter was the Army Pay corps and McTavish said I would be ideally suited to this and to my lowered health category. So I applied and McTavish gave me a strong reference. In due course, with an acceptance and the instruction that I was to follow instructions for transfer back to U.K. which would be issued shortly. After at least one month with no further word on the matter I sent off a signal requesting travelling authority for the movement of Sergeant Bellinger to U.K. for entry into the R.A.P.C O.C.T.U. A signalman came two days later with my movement order. The signalman was Ron Barratt – who had been a member of my class in grammar school. He too survived the war and was involved many years later in a matter concerning his adopted son who had come to work in my final bank branch in Sheffield. He had been caught stealing minor amounts of cash in a stupid fiddle which had been bound to be found out; so very sad for Ron Barrett. Even later after I had retired I saw him in my wife's hairdressers – waiting for his wife. I looked at him and was not sure that I knew him. He had looked at me and made no sign of recognition. After he had left with his wife and I was having my hair cut I asked the barber if he knew the man who had been waiting. He said that it was a Ron Barrett!! He also told me that Ron had been very ill a short time ago and had been on a life support machine for some lengthy period. So much so that it was decided that there was not any hope for him and the life support machine was switched OFF. At which event he made a speedy recovery!!! I therefore think that he did not wish to recognise me because of the embarrassment caused by his adopted son. I wished he had said 'Hello' because he was as straight as a die.

Back to the instructions to transfer back to the U.K It gave authority to travel by rail to Cairo and thence to Port Tewfik where I would embark on the Polish 'Pilsudski' for South Africa. And that was the start of a very long journey. On the train we stopped outside GAZA and I saw three soldiers get off the train who had been wandering all over Palestine ostensibly trying to return to their unit. They had stayed at my Transit Camp and I had obtained travel documents for them to go back to Cairo etc. And here they were again diddling the system by getting off at Gaza. I could not do anything about it so had to 'let it go' but I realised they were doing this deliberately and should have been charged with being absent without leave.

During the war, have I told you of the black Nubian who had anti-tank shells through both thighs, he was sent home "to die" and here he was getting back to his unit having been cured by tribal "witch doctors" who healed his awful wounds with spiders webs and camel dung.

On my way to Cairo from Gaza I did just see the Pyramids briefly and I shared a compartment with an officer who turned out to be a direct descendant of Robert L Stephenson. I was sleeping in the luggage rack at the time and I remember having a very interesting conversation with this young officer. Then I arrived at Port Tewfik and went on board. It was a small passenger boat that had been used by Poland for the
North Atlantic route. It was coal fired, by shovel, by crew members and the temperature in the boiler house was 140 F and they were Scots engineers. We used to send them down bottles of whisky to help them to keep going. We travelled east down the Red Sea until we docked at Aden. While there for several days we had to fill up with 400 tons of coal. This was loaded by hand by several teams of Yemenite labour, and it went on all night. We threw down some spare slices of bread and this caused them to stop work immediately to scramble for the food. There were over 140 vessels of various types in and around Aden harbour.

From Aden we proceeded south in the Indian Ocean. It was very hot and boring and there were Italian Prisoners of War occupying the steerage or lowest deck. They were guarded by a special unit and I had nothing to do with it but we were aware of their presence and would occasionally see examples of their handiwork. Models of ships, cases made out of bits of scrap metal to hold cigs etc. We felt very sorry for them having to live below decks in sweltering heat.

One older soldier who was with us had been a managing foreman for a big public works contractor. He told us some trade secrets of how the various types of big customer were defrauded under their contracts, e.g. where the bill for tools and equipment were classed as extras then they would scrap new and old tools by burying them under a large pouring of cement (where foundations were deep etc.). He could also drink to apparent excess without turning a hair. All his much younger companions would finish up under the table, so to speak, while he remained sober. Eventually we were told that we were shortly to arrive at Durban. As we approached we saw ahead of us the most awe inspiring sight of a huge tornado. It was directly ahead of us and the sea had been sucked up to the sky and it was of huge diameter. I wondered what the captain would do. In fact he steered straight for it and we were suddenly enveloped in wet mist; but felt nothing by way of pitching. Then we were into Durban harbour.

There were quite a number of South African troops on board and they had not been used to the strict discipline of our lads. They had developed a lot of feeling against the very officious Warrant officer in charge. When it came to planning for disembarkation, we were all ordered to bring up our kit bags and store them on deck. (This was before we had entered harbour – still at sea in fact). The Warrant officer suddenly discovered that his own very elaborate extensive kit was missing. It had been pushed overboard in the night and with suitable holes punctured in each case so that they sank. He went berserk. The ship was searched from top to bottom, stem to stern etc. and nothing was found. The Warrant Officer I was utterly distraught.

Everyone was carefully scrutinised as we left the ship. Nothing was found! But I do not think that anyone was charged with its disappearance. He had been in Egypt for a long time and he had obviously acquired some valuable mementos and now it was all lost. In some ways he had certainly asked for it – these colonial troops were on a different wavelength with their own officers, either commissioned or not – they used Christian names throughout, for instance. Once on dry land again we were transported to Dalewood camp – on the outskirts of the town. It was a huge camp of large marquee type tenting with massive tent poles and many beds to each tent. Having settled all our kit bags against each allocated bed, we decided we would like to go into the town, have baths and a decent meal and some relaxation. So my little group organised this and off we set for the big city. First we wanted hot baths and food. So we went to the best hotel we could find and asked for just that. They could not have been more sympathetic and helpful. We were each shown to a wonderful bathroom and given huge bath towels, and we were not charged. Then we went to a penthouse restaurant (12th floor) and we each ordered our individual choice of meal. One very large Irish Sergeant 'Bill' ordered a mixed grill. When it came on a huge oval shaped dish, it had a large steak, a lamb chop, pork chop, two fried eggs and lots of vegetables. The rest of the diners were all South African civilians and they were very interested in us soldiers from the Western Desert etc. When this 'Bill' had finished his large platter of food the waitress came and asked politely if he would like anything else. To everyone's delight and her surprise he ordered 'same again please'. That earned him a great deal of respect.

Another unusual thing we enjoyed was to travel about the town by rickshaw. They were pulled by huge Zulu warriors who wore thick sharks' teeth 'garters' on each leg; they were bare footed; and having got the rickshaw moving would pull a two passenger rickshaw at the run. They had magnificent physiques.

We also attended the playhouse which was a cinema and we saw a film with a famous film star (Dorothy Lamour) whose photograph I was able to record. The amazing thing about the playhouse was the fact that inside the cinema the ceiling was dimly illuminated as though it was the sky. There were stars and drifting whispy clouds, for all the world it was as if it were outside in an open air theatre such as they had in Cairo, very impressive.

One night we came back from a visit to the town and a great wind storm had been raging for several hours. When I got to my bed it was to find that the main tent pole had crashed down. IT WAS RIGHT ACROSS MY BED. If I had been in bed at the normal time, I would have been crushed to death. Spared again I thought!

Durban was a lovely city and the shops, to our war weary eyes were like magic grottos. Bill, the one who had had the double helping, was a single man and was very shy about ladies underwear, but he wanted to buy some luxury undies for his mother. So he went into this wonderful department store with a married sergeant who said he would advise him. At the counter, which was served by a very pretty girl, there were models showing various items of underwear and she asked Bill if she could help. Bill blushed like a teenager, at which stage his friend blurted out that he wanted some knickers for his mother! However when they got down to discussing size, appearance and suitability, and considering that his mother was still only in her young forties, Bill asked the girl what such and such garments would look like. To his surprise and his friends delight the girl said 'Like this' and she unzipped her smock and revealed the most delicate and decorative bikini set in hand embroidered silk. I think he bought the lot!!

I also took advantage of the plentiful supply of lovely clothes and bought a few pairs of American made 'nylons' for Joyce and also two hand embroidered silk pyjamas. They made a wonderful present when I finally got home many months later, because the public austerity in U.K. was very severe and luxury goods were genuinely scarce. The nylons lasted many years with careful use because they were not made to snag and have ladders as I am sure that they were made to do by English manufacturers!

After about six weeks in Dalewood and after making contacts with many very kind civilians who were so hospitable and friendly, we were ordered to start out in a different boat. It was called the Christian Hugens, was Dutch owned, and it had been used on the Holland/Dutch East Indies routes. It was designed for hot countries and had wide promenade decks etc. and it was about 14,000 tons. In this new boat we sailed from Durban to Cape Town, and the ship was our hotel for the period of our stay there. Again it was lovely to see lights everywhere, shops full of lovely things and more or less normal activities, restaurants and theatres. Table Mountain was the dominant feature that I remember and we explored this and the surrounding villages, Petermaritzburg and saw native kraals etc.

We were aware of some hostility from the Dutch crew of the ship. We also noticed that we often had inferior food supplied on the mess deck etc. for example the crew always seemed to be in pairs as though they were not too confident of their safety. I think the ship had stocked up with second-grade food when they knew that they were going to become troop carriers! When we were getting ready to sail it was the day of my birthday, 26th September, 1941 and I was told to be Orderly Sergeant and unable to go ashore. Instead I was given custody of a soldier prisoner who was being transferred to U.K. under strict custody for trial in the U.K. I was told that he had escaped deportation several times already – and not to trust him. So I locked him up and fed him through a trap door. When I handed him over to my relief Sergeant, I gave him some advice, but he fell for his 'blarney' and let him go to the toilet whereupon the prisoner dived over the side and was gone again. It must have been 33 feet to the sea level but he swam ashore with no trouble and escaped, and his jailor faced disciplinary action for his lapse.

As we got ready to set off again news leaked out through the 'grapevine' that we were to take some VIP Air Force Officers to Canada and that as we were a fast ship we would make the journey without escort of any kind. We would be reliant on speed and doing a constantly changing zigzag course. We soldiers had to undertake various duties such as 'ships' watches' on look-out for aircraft and/or submarines or enemy battleships. I did this for some time but then had my duty changed to an inside job. While doing look-out we were in gun turrets with an automatic gun which could swivel in all directions. The turrets were about five feet square and had a shelf like ledge on all sides. It was possible to get some rest using this by placing the head on one side, your back on the next and your feet on the third side. I was able to actually sleep in my off duty periods when they occurred in the night; and I was then always ready at a moments notice in case of need.

It was a wonderful vantage point from which to see the wonders of nature. The sea birds were amazing and would follow the ship day after day without having to flap their wings. They were able to use the air currents caused by the ship, and swooped and dived with tremendous grace and efficiency. The birds were of all kinds including albatross, frigate and many kinds of gull.

Then there were the animals of the sea. Huge whales, sharks, porpoise, flying fish etc. and in Aden harbour I had seen a huge sting ray. It had swum in leisurely fashion among all the ships in the harbour. It must have been 10 feet across.

The ship had a speed of about 14 to 18 knots (from memory) and it had been adequate to do the run unescorted. We sailed west until we were just off the coast of South America and then changed course for the north. We travelled at full speed and it took us 25 - 27 days to finally land at Halifax, Nova Scotia. Here we disembarked our VIP's and learned that we would not start our Atlantic crossing before we had had the ships' portholes all steel welded over, as a safety precaution apparently. For this we had to journey to St. Johns, New Brunswick. It was now November and as we went up the Bay of Fundy it was a pea-souper with no visibility. The ship's siren was being used constantly and we would also hear the warning boom from other ships. However, there were no accidents and we eventually landed in dry dock without incident. It was very cold and sea water could be seen frozen on the shore line. Having come from the heat of the Middle East and the South Africa in their summer, it was very cold to us and we were forced to wear all our warm clothing (we only had tropical kit and uniforms because of where we had been). There were soldiers there who had come south from places like Iceland who felt so warm that they were going about with their coats open or even without them altogether.

Here again the people of St. Johns came to the boat to offer hospitality to our boys and I was taken by my hosts to their home on the first Sunday. Having had a fine meal of venison they said they were Baptists and would be going to church that evening – I could accompany them or stay in their home as I wished. I accepted their offer however and went with them to the service. The preacher wore a full morning dress and was an impressive personality. He introduced me to the congregation and after the service, as we left the Chapel, all the congregation shook me by the hand and wished me well.

On another day a family called MacIntyre picked me up together with a soldier who had been wounded on Crete. He had been shot through the chest and had suffered from a collapsed lung. We got to their house, which I remember was made of wood, two storeys, with a unique central heating system. It was fired by wood and hot air was pumped throughout the house via a double or cavity wall by which the house had been built. They had a son of 16 called Bim, and it was suggested that he should take us duck shooting on the Kannibecasiois River – some distance away. This we accepted and the family car was driven by Bim to where they had a summer house. Again it was built in wood and had a boathouse under the front of the house which came to the river bank. Bim had brought a friend of similar age so there were four of us. They produced two birch bark canoes and a double barrelled shotgun for each of us and a paddle each.

The river was very wide at this point, possibly ¾ to 1 mile across. The ducks had been hunted many times before and when we fired at them they just dived and were not hurt. This went on for some time and then our canoes separated by about a mile when we heard a broadside from the others and then shouts of 'help'. They were obviously in the water – and it was cold water!

We raced for them at top speed and were with them very quickly. It was Bim and the other soldier who were in the water and I was very concerned for the injured man. We got him into our canoe, over the stern and then I got Bim to hold on to the canoe as we paddled for the nearest shore – which was the far side from where we had embarked. Having got the two wet lads ashore I sent the other young Canadian to get the other canoe (which we needed to get back all four of us). And this he did without mishap. The guns had gone of course, but that was a minor matter. Then I collected brushwood and lit a fire with one of the two matches I had accepted from Bim's mother. They were big headed matches compared with our English Swan Vestas and I had remarked on them to Mrs MacIntyre. Anyway the plan worked and the two boys had stripped off their wet clothes and danced around the fire keeping warm until their clothes were dry. Then we set off back home. Bim's mother took it all very calmly and asked me how I felt after the effort of paddling all-out. She seemed to know that I would be having extreme cramp-like aches in shoulders and arms – and she was right. The ache was intense. She bade me to take a hot bath and then proceeded to massage my arms and shoulders with some athletic embrocation. She had obviously done it many times; she was a wonderful masseuse and the awful aches seemed to move down my arms and off the ends of my fingers. When I was having my bath Mrs M had put my clothes in her electric washer/dryer and I had clean clothes to go back with to the ship. They were a grand family and corresponded afterwards. Their eldest son was in the U.K. in the Air Force and had been shot down over Norway and had been able to escape capture and had made his way back to England to resume his service. Later Bim came to U.K. but we did not meet again. I still have a letter from Mrs MacIntyre.

After about six weeks the ship was considered to be ready to sail and it was announced that we would form part of a special Canadian troop convoy to run the gauntlet of the German wolf packs (submarines were looking for and finding many targets in the Atlantic at this time). We finally set off

64

with many ships, some of which were well known huge liners from the P. & O. and Cunard companies' Atlantic service. We were guarded by several destroyers which spent the entire time racing around the convoy looking for German submarines or enemy battle ships. We made a trouble free crossing and my vessel went directly to Liverpool where we spent **four days** waiting to be allowed into actual harbour. It was galling to be kept out all that time after being abroad for two years – more in many cases. But it came to an end eventually. Customs officials came aboard and gave us a blanket clearance so that we were not seen individually on entering the U.K. I was told they had been given back-handers.

From Liverpool it was only a few short hours before I was alighting from the train in Sheffield where I was met by my father and two sisters (2 were otherwise engaged; one nursing in London; one in the Land Army). My youngest sister, Hazel, was there but I did not immediately recognise her as she had grown so much during my time abroad. She was now a grown up teenager and she had seemed to me when I left to be still a child. She had passed the 11 plus exam at the age of 9 (9th in all Sheffield!) and had then been put in a five year stream to slow her down a little; and she asked me how to swot because exams were looming and she had forgotten how to study effectively. So I told her how I did it and she passed with honours in 10 subjects, some three months later. She had always been bright having learned to read and write with her slightly older sisters (she had been able to read and write at the age of three).

The main gift I had taken home from Canada was a complete

ham which had been honey baked. They really enjoyed that. After two days or so I had to report to a unit on the Salisbury Plain to wait posting to the actual O.C.T.U. for the Pay Corps (R.A.P.C.) It was called Bovington Camp and I was there for a few weeks awaiting the final posting to the course which was held at Milford-on-Sea. While at Bovington I had the good fortune to meet and be treated by Stephen Ward, the osteopath who later became mixed up with the politician Profumo. As far as I was concerned he proved to be an excellent osteopath and he corrected the effects of adhesions in my right wrist which had followed a heavy fall on board ship in the Indian Ocean during a gale. He was a very good artist specialising in portraits. And he did two drawings of me after treating my injury. And very good they are. He became involved in Lord Astor's circle and did portraits for many of them. His list of sitters included Prince Phillip, and no doubt the two naughty girls, Christine Keeler and Mandy Rice-Davis, who were also involved. Pity he had to commit suicide. Incidentally, many years later, in the early 1960's I think. I was a witness in a financial case being heard at the old Bailey under Mr Justice Maud, at the time their case was being heard in a main court. I had exposed a fraudster who had taken over one of my customers' business in Derby branch and he went down after the verdict!!! He'd had the temerity to threaten me as well!

From Bovington camp I was duly processed and was directed to the O.C.T.U. which was held at Milford-on-Sea – not very far from Bournemouth. By now it was early 1942 and the course lasted three months. It was winter and very cold. We had a great deal of technical work to absorb and the C.O. was also very keen to balance mental with physical. So we were kept on our toes from reveille to lights out at 9.30 p.m. Every week we had to do a five mile run (in army boots!) and this always followed the best and heaviest lunch of the week – lots of roly-poly pudding! In this particular test of stamina the senior course class was usually fitter than the latest candidates. But when I was there a Jack Selfridge surprised everyone by coming in as the winner when in the junior class. But his face was very red with the exertion. He continued to win throughout his full three months course –he was a genuine 'find'. He came from the Glasgow area and was a member of the British Linen Bank – so we had something in common and were friends to the end of his life – and his family also as they grew up into adults.

One of our officers was a Llt. Miller – neat and athletic and a very strict disciplinarian. His hair was cut very short (back and sides) and the bones at the back of his head formed the shape of a large M. One incident I recall concerned Cadet Russell – another bank clerk – who also came from Glasgow. He was small and felt the cold; he had lost most of his family in an air-raid a short while before. Because of the cold for our outside parade drills he had put on all his available clothing and had topped this with his great coat. He was not much more than 5 feet tall so he finished up as far round as he was tall. At the command to come to the Standing Aim position his rifle was waving about in a very shaky way as the butt was so far from his shoulder, padded as it was by so much clothing. Miller spotted this and grabbed his rifle muzzle, and Russell staggered etc. Miller then told him off and finally said let me show you how to do it. Gave himself the order, having borrowed Russell's rifle, and came smartly to the standing aim position in front of Russell. He then said to Russell 'Now feel my muzzle'. Russell did not hear him correctly or else he did not understand, and slowly moved to Miller's side and felt at his bicep muscle. Miller did not trust himself to control his anger so he dropped the rifle and ran off the parade ground. We were all 'laughing up our sleeves' but we all felt sympathy for 'Jock' Russell.

The following day it happened to be my turn to be the 'Orderly' Cadet. I had to get the whole of my cadet course two miles or so down the road to where there was a short range shooting range. Many of the cadets had never had to use webbing equipment and were very late in being ready to leave our rooms – I had had to 'dress' quite a few. And I took them at the run to try and catch up. We arrived late, for which I got a real slanging from Miller. Then came the actual shooting practise; and he elected to be my coach. As I did my first shots, and they all went within the one bullet hole he suddenly got up, said 'I see you have shot before' and from then on left me alone.

We all passed our exams and were all commissioned as Second Lieutenants and sent out to various Pay Centres – all over the U.K. and some abroad. As I had done two years abroad already I was given a 'home' posting and I was sent to York Paymaster. I was instructed to find private accommodation, this I did in a boarding house beside the railway line, in Grosvenor Terrace. There were several other Pay Corps Officers in this house and they were extremely helpful and friendly.

The fact that we were stationed in a street parallel to the railway line was to prove rather dangerous. The first of the so called 'Baedekker Raids' occurred shortly after I arrived in York. It was at night and the nearest 20 bombs were all within 200 to 400 yards from where I was sleeping in the attic!! The noise woke me up and I dressed hurriedly when I realised what was happening – lots of incendiary bombs floating down; fire starting all around which needed putting out. So I ran down the three flights of stairs calling out to any others who had not heard the raid, but I found that all the upper bedrooms were already empty. They probably did not know that I was in the attic. Then I found them all in the special steel shelter on the ground floor. We had been using it as a table. Anyway I was intent on going outside to see what I could do to help the fire fighting etc. Eventually all was quiet and the raiders were away from their nights work. And it was a great mess. It was fortunate that the cathedral had not been hurt, and as far as I can remember the railway station and main lines were undamaged.

In no time at all I was working with clerks who were keeping account records of a large number of regiments. It was a single entry system – unlike that I was used to in the bank, and there were always possibilities of mistakes occurring which could so easily be missed.

On the 18th July 1942 Joyce and I got married in the Rotherham Parish church. A Cannon married us and most of my family and hers were in attendance. Joyce had managed to buy a beautiful white wedding gown and we left the reception to travel to Goathland where we spent our short honeymoon at the Mallyan Spout Hotel. We were to call there again two or three years later when we had our first born son, John, with us. It was well known for its comfortable rooms and very good food. It was also a very good centre for country walks in lovely scenery. We took lots of photographs which now bring back fond memories.

In the early period of my stay in York Pay Office I had to work in several different locations; old chapels, dance halls; and finally in the factory shop top floor of Rowntrees – the chocolate manufacturers. My good friend Matt Kelly, an Irish officer with whom I got on very well was working in this 'office', when I wasn't. He was a volunteer from Southern Ireland. He was a very good horseman, and knew many of the professional race jockeys. He was once at Pontefract races and had a hot tip. When the horse came nowhere Matt asked the jockey what went wrong. Officially he said it was the saddle that slipped but to Matt he told him that at the last minute the trainer told him "Take him for an exercise only today boy, but the odds will be O.K. at Newcastle next week". So Matt got to Newcastle and won back all his Pontefract losses.

While he was at Rowntrees I asked him if he could get some of their chocolate biscuits so that I could give them to Joyce as a present. He duly came to me with a small attaché case full of delicious 'rationed' chocolate biscuits – at least two dozen I asked him how he had managed it and he said it was very easy. Twice a day all staff could have a cup of coffee or tea plus one chocolate biscuit. He simply ordered twelve cups each morning and afternoon. He had thrown the liquid out of the window to dispose of the surplus. It was on the fifth or sixth floor as I remember it – it was certainly 94 steps up various staircases to get there for I later counted them often. Naturally Joyce was delighted.

Once in an old chapel, we were once again on the 4th floor, I had a civilian lady clerk who was in her mid fifties; she had volunteered to work to help the war, she was a very pleasant lady who had great skill in languages – unfortunately, none in book-keeping and arithmetic. She was in charge of several ledgers of soldiers accounts. The figures involved were not very large but they were in 'old' pounds, shillings and pence. When I inspected her work I was astonished to find that in adding up the columns she had not ever 'converted' the pence into shillings, or the shillings into pounds. This left the accounts in an extraordinary mess. There could be figures which showed pence; a column with more than twelve pence in it and more than twenty shillings in the shillings position. The situation was made more complicated because it was not possible, in war time conditions, to dismiss staff in such circumstances. So I had to gently suggest that she could do a lot more for the war effort by resigning from the Pay Corps and by volunteering for the intelligence corps where her foreign language translation skills would be invaluable. I was successful in persuading her and she left us to sort out the awful state of her ledgers.

At this same 'office' we were visited one day by the Colonel (Cox) who had lost a leg in the first Great War. He apparently told off one of the other young officers in no uncertain terms. As he went out through the door and to the top of one of many staircases, the officer, still smarting from his rebuff, said out loud 'Get gone and I hope you fall down the stairs and break your leg'. There was a tremendous clatter from the stairwell and sure enough 'Corky Cox' had slipped and fallen all the way down the whole flight. We dashed out to see what had happened only to see the Colonel sitting in a dishevelled heap and holding up his separated wooden leg!

Then I was transferred to the section dealing with the accounts of Prisoners of War, and this was located entirely at the Rowntrees factory and this also necessitated a cycle ride to work several miles; and then the 94 steps to 'our' floor. The accounts were split into regiments and there were many thousands of men in these records, mostly of course in German hands. The men were credited with their normal pay and could authorise payments out to wives or parents etc. and their letters were retained as authority. I remember one unusual case where a wife in Liverpool had a family of 18 children – all under the age of sixteen. They had had a first single child; then twins; then 5 (five) sets of triplets. The father was a stage joiner at a theatre in Liverpool – his wife had never been so well off!

There was another course of action that had to be taken when a prisoner found out from his letters from, say, his mother, that his wife had been unfaithful. He was then allowed to put a stop to her allowances. Then when he eventually came home and forgave, we had to put in the "Reconciliation procedure". This required the soldier to appear before his Commanding Officer and swear under oath that he was reconciled with his wife and wished to have her allowance reinstated. The wife, being a civilian, had to appear before a Justice of the Peace and make the same declaration. On one such case the wife sent in the attestation with a letter. The letter said, **"DEAR SER   I HAVE FILLED IN THE FORMS WOT YOU SENT, IT IS ALRIGHT, WE ARE RECONCILED, MY HUSBAND RECONCILED ME**

TWICE ON THE FIRST NIGHT". I had realised that there was an amusing letter because the letter opening secretary had passed it first to one group and then another until all the 'floor' had read it before I got it. Needless to say we restored the payments.

A soldier's mother came all the way from Sheffield with her son's letter of authority for a payment. While waiting for the payment order to be processed we talked. She told me her son had been in Palestine, at this point I admitted I had been there until August 1941. She said "then you must have met him. He is easily recognised he had red hair".

In the early period of our marriage we had rented a 'part house' from a local architect who worked at the Yorkshire Insurance Company in York. We had the use of the lounge and bedroom, and shared the kitchen and bathroom. They had one daughter of about 10 years of age. The husband's name was Ken and his wife was Judith. He was a bit pompous and he was always served breakfast in the dining room. On one occasion he came down to have his breakfast and his wife was busy getting their daughter ready for school. He kept coming out of the dining room and would look up the stairs to see if Judith was about to come down. Finally in sheer desperation we heard him call out 'Judith, are or are you not going to pour me a cup of tea?' Joyce and I could hardly believe it.

They had a cat and it was full of mischief. Joyce, who was nervous of cats would seem to attract its naughty attentions. For example it would jump on to her shoulders from the high point of the stairs and frighten her out of her wits. At

Christmas 1942 we were alone in the house and had bought a small turkey for the Christmas meal. The cat got it, after it had been prepared and was waiting to be put in the oven. I was determined to get rid of the offending animal – without hurting it of course. So I put it in my cycle pannier bag on my way to work at one of the chapel offices. When I got there, to my surprise the cat had managed to jump out, and I did not know where. It never came back and I had to say I did not know what had caused it to disappear!!

Then I had one of my dreams. An old lady appeared dressed in old fashioned clothes complete with bonnet type hat. She told me Joyce was going to have a baby; that it would be a boy; and all would be well. We later found out that she was correct in her statement and from photographs in Joyce's possession; it was her Welsh grandmother I had seen in my dream. So we decided then and there to find a furnished house so that we could have our baby in our own home.

We found a lovely, semi-detached house some three or four miles out of York centre at White Cross Villas, on the Hull road. It was very nicely furnished, had three bedrooms and was owned by a lady who had a vinegar making business. The rent was £2.00 per week. Incredible by today's standards! On the 8th June 1942 John was born there in the front bedroom (we had decided that the hospitals and nursing homes were all too near to railway lines and therefore vulnerable to air-raids).

From time to time, the subject of inoculations would rear its sometimes ugly head. While I was working in a converted Chapel, the Staff Sergeant there was ordered to get all his inoculations up to date as he was about to be transferred to the Indian war zone. When he came back from hospital he said he had been asked if he would like to renew his smallpox jab. He had had it only a short time ago and it might still be effective. However, they told him that it would be an advantage to renew it as he was going to India where the risks were greater. So he accepted and was duly vaccinated in addition to various other protective injections. Before I left that office a few months later we were staggered to learn that the poor old Staff Sergeant had died of smallpox, so much for inoculations. My father had always been against them and I had come to share his views.

Another case about vaccinations occurred a few months before the end of the war. Apparently there had been a growing tendency to refuse to have these protective jabs and the army authorities made a special point of trying to persuade full acceptance. One day all junior officers were called together at the M.O.'s office to have this pep talk which would be followed by the actual injections or vaccinations. It was a female doctor with the rank of Captain. She was very bombastic, very overweight and very put out when all of us refused the injections. This put her in a very bad temper as though it had been a personal slight. She recorded the refusals in our Officers Army Books and then got ready to inject one acceptor, an oldish Captain Riley (who had ribbons from the First World War). He had a slightly withered left arm and it was into this arm that she fairly stabbed her needle. I think it struck the actual bone of his upper arm. He swore loudly at her action, said she need not take it out of him and told her she was a fat old cow.

All this feeling had been engendered by a recent case of adverse reaction to the vaccination of two other young officers, whose arms had swollen with infection, and who had to stay in hospital for over a week. Not only that, but their pay had been stopped as though they had been suffering from venereal disease. One of these two officers was Lt. Ian Plenderleith. His son, also Ian, became a member of the Bank of England Bank Rate Committee in the late 1990's and into 2001.

A few months after John's birth Joyce and I went to visit her parents, whilst there we took advantage of their baby-sitting, to go to see a film at the town cinema. There, we realised later, Joyce was bitten by a poisoned fly at the left side of her mouth; from this there developed cellulitis of the mask (face). By this time, of course, we were back in York and I was on full duty. At first it seemed that Joyce had probably caught 'flu' and the doctor treated it that way. Joyce was still feeding John and it became an ever greater burden and she was in distress. Since the doctor seemed unable to give any other advice or treatment I insisted on having a second opinion – and that meant having her taken to the York Hospital.

The specialist decided it was cellulitis and gave her the latest sulphanilamide drugs. She lost a lot of her hair, her face on the left side became almost purple, and her lips swelled up enormously. The hospital registrar then classed her as being dangerously ill, and gave me the privilege of seeing her at any time i.e. outside main visiting hours. I had had to wean John and he responded as though nothing had happened – he simply went on gaining weight at the same 6½ - 8 ozs per week. I also caused quite a sensation in that I took John to see Joyce in hospital, several miles away, by pushing him in our reconditioned Osnath cream pram and I was dressed in full formal uniform with my Sam Brown belt and cane. I think the troops I passed were very pleased to make me return their salutes. Joyce was in a separate room while in this hospital and had a door into the main ward. She told me that a baby girl had been born in the ward. They had called the baby Pearl. Joyce then discovered that the baby's mother was Mrs Button!!

My family rallied round and two of my sisters, Joyce and Dorothy came and gave their help while Joyce got better. This she eventually did, but it had been a very serious illness, and she might easily have died, as indeed did General Montgomery's wife from the same illness.

There developed a very nice friendship while we were living at this address. It had started some time before John was born. I had gone out for a fast walk one evening and came across a market garden. It was at Langton House, Osbaldwick. It was about 4 acres in extent and I could see over the hedge that it was growing a huge crop of strawberries, and they were getting ripe. Now I knew that Joyce loved strawberries, and I thought that it would be a great tonic to be able to surprise her with such a rare delicacy. So I presented myself at the house in the midst of this market garden and knocked fairly confidently at the red brick cottage door. It was opened by a sweet old lady. Her hair was white and she had a pleasant smile and personality. She was called Mary Metcalf (husband Arthur), I told her my story and she gave me a very gentle but firm 'I'm sorry but they are all booked for sale at the open market in York'. I had to accept graciously, and started to chat about the army and asked her if she had any family in the army or other services. She told me sadly that her only son, Alan, was in the army and had been captured at Dunkirk, and was now a prisoner of war in Germany. I told her that I was officer in charge of Prisoner of War accounts and that her sons' regiment was one I had in my care. I proffered to bring her the latest official news of the son's regiment – we had the latest news at all times from official sources, and I thought she would be surprised and pleased to get ahead of the news published from time to time in the local papers. She then sold me as many strawberries as I could carry and Joyce was able to regale herself on strawberries and cream. Our local farmer had a Jersey herd and we could get bottles full of cream whenever we liked to collect it. In fact I used to make butter on a regular basis – churning the cream by hand in a milk bottle while I read a book. That friendship developed to a lifelong one. We saw Alan come home, as the prisoner camps were over-run and released; saw him get married and in the last few years knew him well as he came to the end of his active and useful life. He became leader of the local council until his death.

When John was about 12 months old I thought it would be a good idea for us all if I could get a tandem bicycle together with a suitable side-car. So we watched the local adverts and eventually found a very acceptable example – buying the side-car separately. John loved it and we became very experienced cyclists. John wore safety straps which allowed him to stand when he felt like it. When this was photographed and shown to a family magazine we were criticised for letting him stand – possibly to his danger. But we were quite sure he was safe and we never had any accidents. On one occasion we had travelled to Pocklington where the Polish Bomber squadron were stationed. We were standing on the road at the beginning of the runway where the latest bomber raid planes were coming to land. I suddenly had a premonition of the danger we were in –that the crews were tired and probably wounded and also flying with damaged controls. I said 'Come on Joyce, we are in danger; pedal for all you're worth' and we did just that. When we were about one mile from where we had been, a bomber plane came down and crashed, just where we had been standing. The blast caught up with us and pushed us quite strongly on our way and we knew that we had been in very great danger and could, so very easily, have been killed.

When John could walk we decided it was time to order a simple pushchair pram, and this we did at Mr Jackson's pram shop. When he eventually called with the new pram we greeted him with great warmth and expressions of pleasure. He told us it was a very different greeting from that which he had received from his last delivery. Apparently he had called at this other address and had seen a lady on the front steps of a terraced house. He called out that he was Mr Jackson and he was pleased to be delivering the new limousine. At this the lady scowled. So he started again more formally and said it was the delivery of the pram that had been ordered from this address. She then said 'I know who you are; I'm not all that pleased; it's for me, I'm 63 and my new baby will be the same age as my great grandchild'. She had a daughter of 39, who had a daughter of 20, who had also just given birth. The case was featured in the paper Reynolds News. (The same paper that had announced the details of the family with 18 children and five sets of triplets).

Our young officer friends were also starting their families, and they followed us with their birth announcements. Jack Selfridge was one, he had a boy David, six months after us; Ian Plederleith had a son Ian (later to become one of the Bank of England's Interst Committee). David Selfridge became a doctor in Lintithgow, near Edinburgh, and we have maintained a happy friendship ever since. Their two lovely, very bright daughters are still in contact and we value their friendship highly.

As most of the German ex-prisoners came home and were returned to their army units the work of the Prisoners of War section of the Pay Corps began to be wound up. Regulations were published as to what would happen when the war finally ended.

I had already found out that my salary on return to the bank would only be about £400.00 per annum. This compared to my pay and allowances as a paymaster in the Army of £1,300.00 per annum from which I was able to save up to £300.00 per annum (In readiness to start putting a home together). In these circumstances I felt I had to give serious consideration to the Army offer of converting my war time commission into a permanent one. So I applied officially so as to be able to find out what other conditions would apply to peace time service.

This started the long process of being interviewed by several War Office Selection Boards. At none of these was I able to put my personal questions as to how peace time service might affect both me and my family.

The final interview was to be with the Northern Command Psychiatrist. I saw him at the York General Hospital. He was set up in one of the hospital corridors. He was a rather portly built Major and was in ordinary Battle Dress. As we met I said I had some urgent questions to which I wanted answers. He said let me 'do' you first and then I will do my best to give you advice as required. So for the next 10 to 15 minutes he asked me all sorts of questions as to my early life etc. He then said "This is the final question, describe your father in one word". I said that is easy, "DRIVER". He said that is good and I will now describe your father to you. And this he did in great detail and as though he had known him.

Then he said do now ask me your questions. I said that I knew what conditions applied in War Time but I was ignorant of what life would be like in Peace Time conditions, and how these would affect my family, wife and children.

He told me that two thirds of the time would be spent in overseas locations such as Germany or elsewhere. When there my life would revolve around the C. O. and also the C.O.'s wife. If I or my wife did not 'cow-tow' to both of them my prospects for promotion etc. would be NIL. Then he said and I can tell you that you would not be able to adopt this role and I would think seriously before going any further with your application. So I thanked him very sincerely; went back to my unit and withdrew my application.

When I rejoined my bank my salary was only £440.00, so we had to manage and we did.

Release from the services was to be based on length of

service, age etc. unless you were classified as Operationally Vital (or some such words). When my own date of expected discharge got nearer I was told that I was to be classed Operationally Vital. There was an appeal process. So I appealed.

After some little time I was ordered to be present when the Paymaster in Chief was to attend in York Pay Office. He would see me personally and study my appeal and its reasons etc. The Paymaster General turned out to be a very understanding man and also a customer of Barclays Bank (my employers) and he listened carefully and sympathetically to all I had to say. He said it seemed that all the very good paymasters were wanting their release while the poor performing ones were happy to stay on. I was able to quote that in York Pay Office I knew of several slap-happy ones who had been released when they were all too ready to stay as long as they could because they had no career to return to – as was not the case with myself. I told him that I had been a T.A. volunteer; had been in the war effort since the end of August 1939, so that I had missed more than six years of bank experience, and that my future could be seriously, adversely affected etc. After pondering for a few minutes only he agreed that he would order my release immediately. And it happened.

We were given the final drill, a medical, civilian suit, farewell payment and a railway pass to our home town. In the days before my departure I had taken the opportunity to go shopping in Harrogate to buy a civilian overcoat and various other items of dress. When I got back to the railway station to return to York, I got there just as the guard was about to wave his flag to start the train. The train was in a bay platform, and there was an elderly gentleman running slowly ahead of me. I asked him if he was for York – he said yes so I held the carriage door open for him and bundled him into the carriage. When he got his breath back he thanked me and said he was nearly 73, and his father of 95 years of age could still run faster than he could. Apparently this old man lived in part of his son's house, read The Times and always walked three miles at least every day and looked like being a centenarian in due course. I thought that was quite a good recipe for long life.

Final release came at last and we made our way to Joyce's parents' home with John and all our baggage, one bicycle, no furniture and lots of memories.

I mentioned earlier the friendship Joyce and I had with Lt. Matt Kelly. I think it would be of great interest to tell a little bit more of this wonderful character. His family were Irish and they had lived in South America, I believe in Argentina, he now lived at New Park Lodge, West Meath, in the Irish Free State. At the start of the war he had volunteered for the army and therefore felt he could wear his favourite type of uniform i.e. riding breeches and riding boots at all times. He always had a twinkle in his eyes; was mad keen on horses, horse racing and target shooting. One of the good events that Matt organised was a short range firing range where A.T.S. girls were invited to attend to try their hands at shooting with Morris-tubed Lee Enfield rifles. This made them .22 gauge and the range at which we shot was thirty yards. One of the A.T.S., a Private Dillinger turned out to be a remarkable shot. From the prone position she could shoot five shots all through the same hole. No wonder her name was Dillinger, the same as an infamous American gunman. The other remarkable fact was that Matt could take off his spectacles and could see the position of each shot as it was made. Private Dillinger was a perfect example of how to compose oneself to achieve extreme accuracy. She stopped breathing and was utterly still prior to the trigger being squeezed. I was most impressed; I had to admit that she was even better than I.

I have already recounted how he obtained the supply of chocolate biscuits for Joyce; well I once asked him if he would be kind enough to bring back some exotic perfume for me to give Joyce when he was next on leave to Ireland. This was immediately granted and he came through Customs and Excise with his pockets bulging very obviously. Apparently the official touched each of these swellings saying 'this is no doubt a wee gift for your dear mother, wife or sister' etc. until he had exposed all the dutiable goods he was carrying. Then he said 'take them by all means with my blessing, you and their recipients deserve a bit of luxury from Old Ireland'.

When John was born he was hugely excited and interested in his progress. So when we were considering John's christening, we thought it would be good if Matt would accept the honour of being one of his God-fathers. At this Matt looked very embarrassed and said he could not accept, much as he would have loved to have been able to accept. The reason was that he was a devout Roman Catholic and it would be forbidden. So I then invited him to attend and join our little party at the church private ceremony. This he accepted, though he said he would have to pay serious penance to his confessor. He duly came and knelt the whole time on the fringe of our party earnestly crossing himself and looking scared.

Then Matt got married to an A.T.S. girl who was working in one of the pay sections. She was not a Roman Catholic, and went through a form of conversion to comply with Matt's Priest's demands. They had a baby girl, Anne, and after the war was over she became a baby in a tug-of-love case. His wife had taken Anne away and gone to live with her mother in Hull while Matt had his home near Dublin. Matt started law proceedings; then felt it would be quicker and more effective to take the law into his own hands, So he laid careful plans, picked up his baby, Anne, and rushed back to the Irish Free state, where he could not be affected by our laws. He brought up his daughter with the help of his two sisters and she was educated in a convent. We had kept in touch with Matt and knew about these circumstances and after we had come to live in Hathersage we were invited to attend Anne's wedding in Dublin. Joyce and I decided to accept and attend the wedding and then continue our stay in Ireland and make a holiday tour so that I could show Joyce some of the beautiful places that I had toured by bicycle with my brother Lol way back in 1934. My car at that time was a Mercedes 230 SL and we shipped it to Dublin from Holyhead without any trouble.

The wedding was fine and we enjoyed the occasion even though Matt surprised me by inviting me, actually at the formal wedding breakfast, to make a speech appropriate to the occasion. Then we had our tour including Killarney, Blarney Castle and the Blarney Stone. I had told Joyce of the custom of kissing the Blarney Stone and the effect it was supposed to have. However, when we got there it was raining hard and there was an American charabanc party of ladies. They were all fulfilling the rites and to do so were being asked to sit on rolled blankets in order to go down backwards to kiss the stone. Obviously when they got up after succeeding in their endeavours, their clothes were saturated and they all walked away tugging at their sodden underwear!

Anne and her husband, J Scanlon (James?) visited us in the following year and then we heard that Anne was not happy about her husband's infidelity and general behaviour. By this time it was early 1970/1 and we had become Spiritual Healers through John's illness. So when we were asked for healing help, Mr Webster told Robert how to do absent healing and suggested that he should carry out this process. Some time later Anne's employers (funeral directors called Flannagan) rang to ask for an actual visit. I was very busy as President of the Sheffield Centre of Institute of Bankers and could not find time to go. So I suggested that Joyce should go with Robert direct to the nursing home near Dublin where Anne was being treated for her nervous breakdown. I should have said that when Robert did his initial absent healing he had 'astral travelled' to Anne's bedside and he had described all details of the room where she was one of five or six female patients. Their beds were separated by furniture, and he had sat on Anne's bed and given her healing. When Joyce and he had got there it was to find the room was exactly as Robert had described it. Quite remarkable and just one of many proofs we have received of Spiritual Gifts.

Sadly, there was to be a tragic final outcome. We heard some time later that Anne had taken her own life. It must have broken Matt's heart and we did not hear from him. We were left with many memories and were only sorry that there was not a happy ending. Joyce and I had very much enjoyed our holiday at the time of the wedding, and Matt had been thrilled to travel in the 230 S.L.

After the War had ended

After the first feelings of freedom on discharge from the army the pressures of living in the home of my in-laws became ever more difficult. There was the kindly meant 'help' with the bringing up of our first born John! So it became a matter of urgency to find a home of our own. Through the advice of a longstanding friend I heard of some newly built houses that had been sanctioned for immediate erection because the foundations had been put in before the war at which point further progress had been stopped because of the war effort and the rules that had been adopted to conserve everything for the advancement of the country's war needs. The row of houses was in Barnecliffe Crescent in Fulwood, Sheffield. They were in a very high, even exposed position, but the views were lovely in all directions. One of the main advantages of being employed by a bank was the fact that the staff could borrow money for essential house purchase at the very low rate of 2½% interest. In addition the loan could be for 95% of the purchase price. So we bought our first house and were very happy.

At this time, my father was living alone as my mother had left with her mother during the latter part of the war, when Granny had had a disagreement with my father. She said she could no longer put up with him and was going to return to her own home in Workington (she was always a very independent strong minded lady). Mother said she could not see her old mother going off alone at her age of over seventy, in all the difficulties caused by the war conditions, so she would accompany her and look after her for the rest of her life, and this is what she did.

Granny died in the last few months of the war. We were still in York and we heard all about this from my sister Dorothy after the event. Apparently she had helped mother over Granny's death and funeral arrangements and had also taken furniture and other items she fancied. One example of this was an old elaborate clock that was covered by a glass dome. I only knew of this some years later and reminded Dot that this had been mentioned in Granny's will as being left to me. Dot agreed and handed over the clock complete with its dome. After a few months I decided that I did not really need the clock and so I returned it to Dot on my next visit.

After some time I was doing quite well in my progress in the bank. I had been on several refresher courses run by the bank to bring service men up to date with current practice. This had meant several stays in London while attending at Wilberforce's house in West Wimbledon (it was he who did much to stop the slave trade with African slaves to America). Then in early 1947 we were having a very severe winter with very heavy falls of snow and with this we had strong easterly winds which caused drifting which was so bad that all downstairs windows were covered and the snow reached to the roof on many occasions.

The bank asked me if I would be prepared to attend Manchester Foreign Branch for a period of three months so that I could become the Foreign Business expert for the Sheffield region branches. Joyce would be left without my assistance throughout the week and we had no telephone, but it would be possible to return home every weekend. So it was agreed and I had some very good experiences on this specialist side of banking.

Shortly after this was completed Joyce and I became increasingly aware of the shortcomings of our home. The kitchen was supplied with a back-to-back oven, this was heated by the fire in the adjoining dining room and it was all too easy to forget to fuel the fire in the other room. So I got a customer builder to remove the oven and supply an electric oven in the kitchen and a separate electric radiator in the dining room. There was an unexpected reaction to this from our previously friendly neighbour, Peggy Haigh. She was incensed that we had made our house better than theirs without telling them of our plans. She would not speak to Joyce from that day onwards. I found it hard to believe that anyone could react in such a way. I was reminded of the old Yorkshire saying 'There's nowt so queer as folk'.

Early in 1947 Joyce had decided that she was feeling very much better; she had felt below par since the serious illness she had suffered in York (Cellulitis of the face). She now felt it would be possible to start a new pregnancy. When we knew she was pregnant we felt sure that it would be a girl and decided that we would call the new arrival Pamela Jean. Some short time later my father sold his house and started to live with one or other of his locally living children. This started with us. A silly little thing upset him and he then upset Joyce – so much so that she suffered a miscarriage.

I felt it was important that she should build up her health and took her to a lady osteopath, Miss Braum, and she gave her several manipulations. She found evidence of a childhood accident when Joyce had fallen off a moving tram and corrected misalignments in her neck and pelvis. Headaches which had been frequent stopped and she began to feel really well once more. So we started a fresh pregnancy and this time all was well and Robert Edward was born at home on 18th July 1948 (also our wedding anniversary). When he was born the doctor said he was covered in white grease, the first time he had seen this since before the war, and he was very vigorous and healthy.

When the birth was over it was necessary for me to go shopping in Sheffield. So leaving Joyce with her new baby and an adult sitter I took little John with me to Sheffield which involved two separate buses. On our way home, burdened with my many purchases we got to the half-way stage where we had to change to the final bus, only to be just too late so that we just missed the connection. I was quite upset and muttered words of exasperation. Whereupon John tugged at my trouser leg and said in his gentle way "Don't worry Alan, there will be another one soon", very typical of John's permanently calm philosophical attitude to life. He is still the same!

It was at this juncture that we had the idea that we should consider selling our house; leaving us without accommodation and thereby enabled to apply for planning consent to build our own new house. We found a desirable site in a truly rural small complex called Shatton, near Bamford in Derbyshire's Hope Valley. It was a half acre piece of ground with a stream running at its rear boundary. It was owned by Peter Priestley – famous for his sheep dog handling – so we sold our house and made almost 100% profit! We had intended to rent accommodation but Joyce's mother said she would be mortally offended if we did not stay with them again. We gave way thinking it would not be very long before we had our own new house and duly made application for consent to build.

The planning authority was at Chapel-en-le-Frith and the Planning Officer was the Water Engineer. He turned down our application on the grounds that private developments had to be one tenth of Council developments and in that area of Shatton it was already the other way round.

So there we were back at Joyce's mums and no prospects of a new house. Then the Bank stepped in, knowing that we were not committed to a house they decided to move me to Doncaster Branch. While there as security clerk cum cashier I met an old fellow class mate from my grammar school days. He was the assistant architect to the Borough Council and suggested that I should be guided by him and build a new bungalow near to where he himself had built at Bessacarr, just off the main road to Bawtry. We saw the site and agreed to follow his advice, which of course included the planning and supervision of the building.

Applications to the council were approved and the bank agreed the necessary loan and we were off on the exciting new development. The new bungalow was ready for occupation in early December 1949 and we moved in on the 10th and started planning the half acre garden which had been part of a very large agricultural field which had been under cultivation. One week later, much to my utter amazement and chagrin the bank surprised me by asking me to transfer back to Fitzalan Square Sheffield branch to take up a promotion to Security Clerk in this bigger branch. In the circumstances I told the District Manager that I would be happy to make the transfer to the new branch by travelling daily by bus if they would pay the five shillings a week travel expenses. They said "No" to that and so I had to forego that promotion. The next time I was offered a much bigger promotion was four years later to be Chief Clerk of the Local Head Office in Sheffield with the District Manager being my immediate boss. He was called Tom Speet and he had come from the Manchester area via Bradford main branch. This time I accepted and that set in train all the ususal preparations for a house move.

I had learned a great deal under the Doncaster Manager whose name was George Widdowson. He had come to Doncaster branch to replace Frank Swindells who had been promoted to be manager of High Street Sheffield Branch. Widdowson was a tremendous business getter and made Doncaster branch expand rapidly and considerably. He made great contacts through people he met in the local public houses and bars. His wife Mary was dismissive of these contacts but whenever she started to nag him George would promptly go to sleep and leave her frustrated and finally speechless. It was very funny to see it happen.

On one occasion I had gone at night with George and a motor dealer called Tommy Wroot to a farmer who lived out in the Lincolnshire Wolds. The plan was for Tommy to sell the farmer a nice second hand car and for George to lend the farmer the money with which to buy it. The farmer's wife realised what was going on and decided that she ought to accompany her husband as George and Tommy took him out to test the car and give him some drinks at the local in order the more easily to persuade him to make the purchase. I therefore was asked by the wife to stay and look after her two small children, who were in bed, and this I readily agreed provided I could just telephone my wife to tell her that I would be late home and that she should not worry and in fact should go to bed and not wait up for my return. Joyce told me that Mary had been on the telephone asking where George was and advising her not to stand for any late nights from me!

When the party finally returned from their outing, the wife had been able to advise her husband not to commit himself and we returned home. As George dropped me off I told him that he would be met by quite a reception from Mary. In the office next morning I asked him what had transpired on his return home. He smiled and said that his dear wife Mary had started to harangue and nag him but he had just got into bed told her to "bloody well shut up" and had then promptly gone to sleep, leaving her frustrated, speechless and stressed. No wonder she had problems in later life with high blood pressure.

There was a funny occasion with his son, Howard, when one of his old Head Office colleagues came to stay with him for a few days. Apparently the conversation had got on to their son Howard and his new school – the Doncaster Grammar School for Boys. Apparently the Armbristers had a friend whose son was also at this same school. Howard said he had a photograph of the Rugby Team of which this boy was a member. So Howard brought out the photograph and showed it to them. When they failed to identify their friends' son they asked Howard to point him out. Howard promptly pointed to a particular boy on the snap and said "It's 'im thee-er wi' 'is gob oppen" and when he arrived in Doncaster only six months earlier his speech had been very correct, even posh, having lived in the exclusive town of Carshalton.

I remember another humorous item from this branch. The chief cashier was called Edmond Horsfield and he took his duties very seriously and efficiently. One day he came back from the counter where he had an elderly customer. The chief clerk was not available so he spoke to me and said he had old Mr X at the till and he was asking for the balance of his account, some £2,000 to be paid to him in cash. In those days this was a lot of money. So I asked him if the old man was known i.e. there was no doubt about his identity and Mr Horsfield said he knew him well, but did I realise that this man was 98 years old. So I suggested that he could show the customer into the Manager's room where I could see him and put the bundle of notes into a canvass 'copper' bag; tie it up and put a loop of the fastening round his wrist; Mr Horsfield thought that this would be a good idea and the customer was shown into the Manager's room where I was waiting. I greeted him and then suggested that he should take a seat – touching him on the arm as a friendly gesture. He promptly shrugged me off and said he could manage to sit down "by me sen" – he was only 98! So I fixed him up as suggested and off he went. Two hours later when I was shopping in the open market I saw the old man still going the rounds of the stalls – the 'copper bag' was still under his left arm. Two weeks later he died – having distributed his money to the various members of his family who had worked with him on his market garden business.

Another memory from that time concerned the chief clerk.

He was a big man named Rouse. He had a slightly bullying manner with the staff who mostly held him in awe. One day I decided to see if he would respond to my belief that all bullies were basically cowards. We were both early for work and he was opening the day's post. I looked at him with a very concerned expression on my face and asked him if he was feeling well. He stopped his letter opening and asked me why I had asked. So very seriously I told him that I thought he looked quite ill, and was he perhaps sickening for something. He dropped what he was doing and dashed for the lavatories. When he came back his face was quite green and he said I was right and he would have to go home until he felt better. I had proved my point but then I had to do his work as well as my own – so perhaps it served me right.

There was another strange fact about Mr Rouse, he could not resist a bargain or a deal which he thought was a very good buy. For example he once saw an advert for some high quality Royal Navy Battleship grey paint. He could hardly wait for pay day (the 23rd each month) so that he could go along to the distributors and buy a whole load of this paint. He would do this every month – each month having a new bargain. His house must have been full of unwanted goods. His poor wife was never smartly dressed and would always attend staff functions in old and dowdy cloths and shoes. Some years later I heard of a similar case affecting the chief clerk of Berwick-on-Tweed branch. Here the fixation or phobia was so severe that the man's salary was always paid out to his wife so that she could control their spending. If left to his own control he would very likely spend it all on the first night buying drinks for all and sundry in the local; all very strange.

At George Widdowson's suggestion I applied for the chance to attend an instruction course, run by Head Office on the Interpretation of Balance Sheets. That meant 4 to 5 weeks in London with home visits at each weekend. It was a very good experience which was of great benefit in the future. Lots more courses followed from time to time and eventually on some of the courses I went as instructor or marker.

The Assistant General Manger in charge of this enterprise was John Tonkin; he was head of the Inspection Department; Examiner to the Institute of Bankers; and to crown it all he had a very highly developed sense of humour and a wonderful memory for names. At one lecture at which I was a student, he was speaking of the occasions when it might be appropriate to assume that a customer was in need of protection of the Trustee in Lunacy. For example, he had been asked by a manager to pass judgement where a lady customer would take out her dentures while talking to you and place them in your hands, then after a short time would take them back and replace them in her mouth; all the time without saying anything about the teeth. Another example was the case of a wealthy elderly male customer who started coming into the bank and drawing out cash of several hundred pounds – several times a week. The branch, he said, did not know whether he was spending the cash or even using the notes as toilet paper. At this point a student, Rowland Hibbins of Sheffield, stood up and said there is a simple way in which you could have been quite sure that he was not so using the notes. "Oh", said Mr Tonkin "How?" Hibbins said they could have issued crisp new notes. There was a roar of laughter, and Mr Tonkin used that Mr Hibbins as an instructor from then on.

The move to Sheffield came about in 1954 and we were determined to find a house somewhere in the Derbyshire countryside. After a very long search we found a very nice semi-detached house in Grindleford and set about making a few essential alterations. We were helped by the same friend who had found us the Barnecliffe house at the end of the war. The house needed a retiling of the roof; new bathroom and separate toilet and finally redecorating throughout. That part was done very well by a professional firm – customers of Doncaster Branch called Singleton. Grindleford was and still is a very beautiful village set in very picturesque countryside and it was connected to Sheffield by a good railway service. Here the boys went to the local school and John started to show his natural inclination towards gardening. This was a great pleasure to Grandad Turton (Joyce's father) for his true hobby was gardening in all its forms and a regular prize winner in his allotment society in Rotherham.

After three years or so at this branch the Bank decided to take advantage of the retirement of the District managers of Local Head Office Sheffield and Leicester to make an amalgamation of those two offices and with that at Nottingham.

They also decided that it would be essential to transfer me to Nottingham – as joint chief clerk in order that my knowledge of the old Sheffield area would be 'downloaded' to the Local Board in Nottingham. In that case I asked if there was any intention to promote me as manager in the near future, because if such were the case then it would be sensible to save an unnecessary house move and all the costs that would entail. To my great joy they agreed that I could expect early promotion, and so I travelled to Nottingham every Monday morning and stayed in local hotels until Saturday mornings, to return home every weekend.

After less than six months they were pleased to promote me as Manager to Markets Branch in Sheffield; and so I did not need to move house or schools for a further period in this idyllic village. This small branch had always been classed as having no prospects of expansion. It was established in the single storey remains of the old Corn Exchange and was on the edge of the Wholesale Markets for fruit and vegetables.

There were many wonderful characters to be met in this community of market traders and their employees and hangers on. I met one such at the premises of one customer, who told me of this man's lifestyle. Apparently he lived in doss houses and all his possessions were 'on his back' He lived on a weekly cycle starting on Monday mornings with no money at all. He would then borrow a few pounds with which to buy a basket full of nosegays or other cheap flowers. Armed with these he would position himself outside the best department stores and sell his wares to passers-by. With this money he would invest in more flowers and carry on to the end of the week by which time he had accumulated enough money(as much as £60) to travel (by platform ticket) to Manchester where his girlfriend lived. He would spend all his money there and come back to Sheffield on the Monday morning – again by platform ticket as he would have no money left. He had been regularly charged in court for misdemeanours and had logged up more cases than anyone else in Sheffield. At the time I first saw him in my customer's stall I noticed that he had many white scars down both cheeks; so I asked my customer, Mr Hall, how these had been caused. The reply was 'by razor slashes' from the lawless people with whom he mixed.

Another example of the strange lives of this fraternity was again customers of the same Mr Hall. This time he had been approached by 'Dixon Lane Sellers' (this was a short road where the traders would assemble to sell inferior goods cheaply). They were not supposed to be there and had to carry their goods in big baskets hung by straps from their shoulders. However, they would often ignore the rules and actually have portable stalls where they displayed whatever they had found to sell - such as tomatoes that were too big, too ripe, old lettuces etc. Mr Hall had been asked "'ave yer got owt for sale?" he had just received twenty small barrels of green grapes that were packed in cork chippings that had been delayed in delivery, so much so that they had turned black. So they did a deal and away they went. They came back the following day and asked if they had any more of those lovely grapes. Mr Hall asked them how they had disposed of them and was told that they had been bagged up in brown paper bags weighing a pound each, then they had taken them to two different theatres where they had sold them to unsuspecting people queuing for tickets. They would then eat them in the dark and probably not know that they were past their 'sell-by-date'.

Another case was told to me by the manager of the Midland Bank whose premises were next door to mine. He had a similar customer who told him that he had thought of buying a new car – in fact an Armstrong Siddely which had had its price dropped by one thousand pounds. He did not need an overdraft, when he turned up with it to show his bank manager he was told that he had exposed himself to being caught by the Inland Revenue for non-disclosure of profits. Whereupon the wide boy said "not me brother, I got a discount from the dealer of sixty pounds with which I bought a used winning tote ticket which showed a win of two thousand pounds – enough to cover the cost of the car". And he just laughed, winked and said that was "one up over the tax boys".

With my methods of contacting many sources of new business I had effectively quadrupled the business and its lending's within six months. Thus proving that I had the ability to find new accounts and do so without losses.

The following spring Joyce and I decided to take a holiday touring in Scotland. I had bought a small new car from the profits of my Doncaster house sale and with camping gear it would not be very expensive. So off we went via Edinburgh where we stopped long enough to see the Castle and other sights. It was while we were driving slowly down the Royal Mile that we were involved in a slight accident. It involved a small boy who had started fighting another small boy. He suddenly ran backwards off the pavement straight into my path. I slammed on the brakes and stopped almost dead but only after hitting the boy whose head had made a dent in the centre of the car's bonnet. He seemed none the worse except for a lump on the back of his head. I asked the women who were around to call the police. They came very quickly and said they wished to check my car's brakes and they sent the boy, (aged about six or seven) to hospital for checking. So Joyce and my two boys John and Robert were put into the police car to wait for my brake test to be completed. Two policemen got into my car; one in the back seat, to confirm it was safe to stop and one beside me. I was to drive down the Royal Mile until I was given the command to stop. I was then to do an emergency stop. We set off, the command was given and I slammed on the brakes. The policeman who was in the front seat, was sitting partly sideways and of course not wearing a seat belt (as would be the case now); the car's brakes were very efficient and he slammed his head on the inside of the windscreen. When he had recovered from the shock he had given himself he said my brakes were very good and accepted that I had been unable to avoid hitting the small boy and there would be no further action. But Robert had seen the accident coming and had a bad headache for some time from shock.

While in Edinburgh I had made contact with the Paymaster General in Chief R.A.P.C Brigadier Bill Taylor under whom I had spent some time in the army reserve of officers. He was stationed in the Castle and had an army house in Edinburgh. He invited us to call and stay with them at the end of our holiday and also take advantage of their tickets to view the final night of the Edinburgh Tattoo from their box seats. This we did and I will tell you of this later.

From Edinburgh we travelled north through many of the well known beauty spots, camping where we found special interest. We were soon in Inverness and from there we turned west until one day we found ourselves in a little place called Badachro – not far form Loch Torridon.

Here we got permission to erect our tent in an area covered by flowering bluebells. It seemed such a shame to put our ground sheet over the top of these lovely blooms, but there was no possibility of avoiding them. It was while camping here that I had those successive nights' dreams of which I give an account in the chapter on Dreams.

The time of year was mid to late June and the daylight seemed to last to midnight. One night we went along to Red Point to fully appreciate the fantastic sunset. I started taking photographs at about 10 p.m. thinking that the colour would soon start to fade. But the wonderful sunset went on and on until after midnight. I used up two whole spools and they fully justified the expenditure. I used to use two Leica cameras – one for contact prints, the other for transparencies which later could be projected and thereby enlarged on to a silver screen. They provided very good memories long after the holiday was over.

When we got back to Edinburgh we were warmly welcomed by Bill and his wife Eve. They took us into their lovely home and sent us all off to have baths and to tidy up. We came down to a wonderful meal. The main item was an omelette of generous proportions which we later found had been made with 36 eggs! It was served on an oval silver salver. We were hungry and had been living mostly on camp-cooked simple meals. To us it was absolutely scrumptious.

Later we grown ups went to the Castle to see the final performance of that year's Edinburgh Tattoo. Our box was next to the Royal Box and the view was superb. It was a night and performance to remember.

Bill told us a true story of the visit, to their Offices Mess in the Castle, of Lady Mary Malcolm. She was very well known as a BBC personality, newsreader and presenter. The story she had told concerned the transfer of a young officer of the RAPC who was told to have all his injections brought up to date as he had to be transferred to an Indian Command – in fact to the area of the black and yellow-banded snake. He was repeatedly warned that it was particularly poisonous. At every point of contact with knowledgeable officials on his way to India he would be told very similar warnings about this snake. When he finally arrived at his remote station his new Commanding Officer again told him to beware. This snake was very aggressive and would attack if given half a chance. So, what was the correct action to take? As everyone else had said, the only thing to do was to grab the snake by its tail and slide your hand along its body until you had it tightly held, just behind its head. He vowed he would be very careful and would remember all the instructions.

A few days later he was walking down one of the prepared 'rides' through the nearby forest when horror of horrors he saw this long black and yellow banded snake, remembering what he had been told he sprang into action seized the tail end in his left hand and ran his right hand up he tail as instructed. When he was next visited in hospital he was heavily bandaged and only his eyes could be seen of his face. When asked what had happened he explained that having done what had been advised he suddenly found the thumb of his right hand up the bottom of a real live tiger; apparently she told it very well indeed and it went down very well with all present.

Bill Taylor had gone into the war as a Chartered Accountant, made the transfer to permanent commission and shortly after this occasion was promoted to Paymaster-in-Chief. When he retired he went to live near Winchester where we visited for weddings and special occasions.

Having returned from this holiday I got back to my branch to learn that my Local Directors had been asking for me while I was on holiday. They had not been able to contact me as; of course I was not at any known address with telephone etc. So I went immediately to Nottingham and as reported in my Dream Chapter they said all the things as per the dream characters.

As a result of all this I was soon on my way to Head Office for serious interviews and the prospect of promotion to the major branch of St James Street, Derby. It happened; and in 1958 we found a house in the better part of north Derby where we were to live for the next 6½ years.

John who had always displayed a love and understanding of plants and gardening generally was apprenticed to Derby Parks while Robert attended another council school. He did not pass his 11 plus exam for grammar school and therefore ended up at a nearby secondary modern, where he started off in the 'A' form. However, he rapidly descended to the 'C' form in a matter of a few months. At an evening meeting for parents and teachers I asked the Headmaster why he thought that Robert was doing so badly academically. He said "That's simple; he's too secure". You being a bank manager gives him the idea that he does not have to worry about his future etc. So I told Robert that he would have to depend on his own efforts to make his future secure, that he could not rely on his parents leaving enough for him to live on as an adult etc. In three months he was back at the top of the 'A' form.

Not only that but he was soon to receive commendation and appointment as a prefect and later again for handing out discipline to an unruly trouble maker who had stepped out of line when Robert was taking a 'crocodile' to the town swimming baths. He did his homework while going to school on roller skates! But he was very good on current affairs and could hold conversations with adults on any subject and hold their attention as though he were an adult and an equal.

The business in Derby had been run by a Mr Dickinson who had done much of his work from the lounge Bar in St James Street, with a drink in his hand. He had 'lost' a great many accounts annually due to neglect, and it was my job to restore the business.

This I did very quickly and within six months I had quadrupled the lending's. Among other major accounts I got that of Royal Crown Derby Porcelain removing the then chairman in the process.

By the end of my term there I had increased the staff; made a new branch building and had put on accounts at the rate of net gain of 840 per year. Staff had increased to a total of 38 and I had been given an Assistant Manager.

By that time John was working as a gardener and had completed an apprenticeship with Derby Parks, and had gone on for two tears to Pershore Horticultural College. Robert had finished school and had finally chosen to become an Estate Agent and to study to become a surveyor (articled to Allen and Farquarhar!).

I was then promoted to become manager of the main business branch in Sheffield, Fitzalan Square, where I had served just before and immediately after the war. This was the middle of 1965. When I left Derby I heard for the first time that the other bank managers had called me 'Skull and Crossbones Bellinger' and I had repeatedly been the branch that made the most progress of any (60 or so branches) in our Local Head Office area.

During my time in Derby I became the President (see photograph) of the Derby Area Institute of Bankers and also a Committee member of the Institute of Bankers. This latter appointment entailed attendance in Lombard Street for Committee meetings every two months or so. I was also appointed a Fellow of this Institute for my services to the Banking Profession. Hence I could put F.C.I.B. after my name. (See also story of seeing Ted Fricker on one of these visits).

Another little story that I have remembered that relates to the time I was in Derby. One of my successes there was to acquire the account of the very prestigious company Crown Derby Porcelain. The Sales Director was a Mr Colin Osbourne – a very nice gentlemanly person. He told me about the love of this company's 'Imari pattern' china that the gypsies felt. They all had it in their caravans; it was a sort of status symbol. He had been collaborating with the Sales Director of the big department store in Manchester called

Kendal Milnes in a special display of their finest china –
including a large proportion of the highly decorated **Imari.**

While they were looking at the special display cabinet with
its special contents they were approached by an elderly
couple who were obviously gypsies, they asked how much
did they want for all the goods that were on display. The
Director said he had not worked it out as a price for a 'job
lot'. At this the gypsy said I'll offer you one thousand
pounds for the lot – Is it a deal? After some hesitation the
Director agreed that he would accept the offer. At this the
gypsy said 'in that case please get it packed up for tomorrow
morning and I will be here with the cash to collect it.

Colin was sufficiently interested to ring his contact the
following day to see what had happened. He learned that they
had not thought too seriously about the deal and had doubted
that the man would actually turn up. But he had and asked
why the china had not been packed up for his collection. They
had got out of the embarrassment by saying that they had
thought he would like to have luncheon in their restaurant as
their guest while they packed the special parcel. Incidentally
the man had arrived with a brown paper parcel under his arm.
It contained the sum of £1000 in notes. Colin said they not
only showed the china off for all to see but they actually used
it on a regular basis not withstanding the high cost.

Fitzalan Square Branch, in the centre of Sheffield was where
many of the old steel industries banked and had a good
reputation for business. It was already planned to be rebuilt
on a very close-by site and this process began as I took over.
The new branch was to have VIP status with lifts, escalators,

special strong rooms for the branch and one as a central reserve, and two assistant managers plus a live in caretaker in atop floor flat. This was going to be my last move in all probability so we were determined to find a house where we could enjoy the countryside. We started looking in Grindleford, where we had lived in the mid 50's but there wasn't a house to be found.

Finally we found one in Bamford which overlooked the golf course called Sickleholme and agreed a price. Spencer's the agents, however, decided they were going to try to get it higher and tried to gazump me. So I withdrew immediately and we all walked along Hurstclough Lane towards Gatehouse Hamlet where our friends told us there were some Beagle's and Corgi's breeding kennels. Just short of these kennels we saw, through some hedges, the house we eventually bought and have lived in ever since.

It was called Gatehouse Farm and was built in 1641. It had a total area of about 11 acres with 9½ available for grazing. (It had been also an Inn for wool carriers who took their bales by mule to Bradford resting or refreshing themselves and their steeds which were tied up at the terrace at the front of the house). The property had been bought at auction in 1958 for £2,900 by a father and son 'Lee' who spent seven years reconditioning and altering, and that is when we saw it. Joyce said "Now this is what I would like" and I said "you shall have it my dear". After that we got into the house and saw its great possibilities. I went about the purchase straight away and finally bought it at £13,750. It needed completing as to floors, kitchen, lights etc. but it was a very good find – and all because we had been gazumped; so lucky!

At this point I feel I should digress to tell of an occurrence that was to have some importance at a few years hence. As manager of the Derby Branch I had become the President of the local branch of the Institute of Bankers. I was also appointed to be the Institute of Bankers Committee Member for the Derby area. This would entail trips to Lombard Street for meetings in Institute Head Office every two or three months. I had heard from friends we used to meet in the Lake District while on holiday, of a man called Ted Fricker. He was a Spiritual Healer, so called, who had successfully treated our friends grand-daughter after an accident which had resulted in concussion and a bad headache. The doctor had confirmed that there was no fracture and advised that the headache would go naturally. When this forecast did not seem to be working they took their daughter back to the doctor for further advice. He again told them to be patient and that it would go in due course.

As they were leaving the waiting room, somewhat disconsolately, an old local lady said they ought to take the child to see a Mr Fricker. He was a butcher who lived quite close, and he was a healer who would be able to help. So they did and she was told that after the Hands on Head treatment the ache would disperse and be completely gone before they got home. And this was what happened. It so happened that while this was happening, the girl's mother was in hospital for the umpteenth time with a mysterious malaise (M.E.) so when she came out of hospital – not any better, she also went to see Ted Fricker. He told her she would have to come three times, after the three treatments she said "I feel so well, if this is good health I've never felt it before".

So I was very intrigued and determined that I would try and meet this special man who could do the things that I, until then, had thought only Jesus could achieve. So I made an appointment to see him at 10 a.m. at his home in North Tottenham on the day I had to travel to London on a Committee day where meetings started at 2.30 p.m. I got there at 10 a.m. feeling that it would give me plenty of time to keep the Institute appointment at 2.30 p.m.

When I arrived at the Healer's home in a little cul-de-sac in North Tottenham I was surprised to find his waiting room almost full with only a few spare seats left vacant. I realised that I would have to wait my turn and that my supposed 10 a.m. appointment was only a guide. I determined to wait as long as I could, provided that I could leave in time for my official appointment in Lombard Street. I think it was my turn at about 12 o'clock and I went into his kitchen where he did his healing.

He was a big man with very dark hair, round glasses and a friendly personality. He asked me what was wrong with me 'young man' and I felt better straight away! I told him that I had injured my back some 16 years earlier while living in Doncaster, I had been lifting heavy flagstones and a severe strain in the sacroiliac area of my spine had been caused.

He put his left hand on my left shoulder and his right hand on my lower back while we were both standing. I was still wearing my winter overcoat and I could feel his hand vibrating right through my body – even though his hand was still. Within a few moments he said that I was now better and was there anything else? So I told him that I did suffer from

111

fairly frequent migraine headaches which would occur as often as every month. When they came on they were preceded by blurred vision followed by intense headache, sickness and diarrhoea, and I would have to go to bed and rest for a minimum of 10 to 12 hours. He said it was not my liver that was causing the problem (as I had thought might be the case) but a nerve pressure. He them 'wiped' his hand over my eyes, then the back of my neck and then my shoulders. He then said that was finished. I thanked him, felt very mentally 'moved' and did not give him anything. I later sent him a donation and bought his book with my thanks.

I then attended the committee meetings and finally caught the 6.30 p.m. train back to Derby. I was travelling 1st class in a compartment with two other men. They were occupying the opposite corner seats, and I was sitting in the centre of the opposite seat facing the engine. Suddenly and completely 'out of the blue' some force took me by the ankles and lifted my feet almost to the ceiling of the carriage. I lost contact with the carriage seat; the other two occupants looked askance at my contortions. I could not possibly achieve what had happened by my own efforts. I was promptly lowered to a sitting position and I felt odd; got up and walked the corridor for a time. I can only report that it was a very strange experience, and more to the point, my back was better and I have not had a migraine headache since.

In the following years it was to prove to be a very important event. For some time I had been noticing that John's thigh muscles had seemed to be wasting; and I had referred him a few times to our Herbalist osteopath friend of Doncaster days. He had always reassured me that there was nothing untoward and I was not to worry about John's health. However, in 1966 he was very much weaker in these and other muscles and I again sent him to see Wilfred Morley (the herbalist). By then I was in Sheffield managing the Fitzalan Square Branch. Wilfred phoned me while John and Joyce were still with him to say he had bad news. I had been right, there was something wrong with the muscles; it was Muscular Dystrophy. It was very serious and I would have to take him to the doctor and let orthodox investigations take their course.

John was 23 years old and had just started work near Shrewsbury in a market garden, which concentrated on tomatoes, cucumbers, lettuce and other quick vegetables. He had completed a gardening apprenticeship with Derby Parks, and followed that with two years at Pershore Horticultural College.

The prognosis was not encouraging; it was a progressive disease; it had no know cure; there was no treatment under normal medical practice; and it was inherited. When I told the specialist that there were four generations alive on both sides of the family with no case of the disease he then changed his definition to 'sporadic'. They seem to have to put a name to it!

John was obviously shaken with the thought of what lay ahead. I comforted him by saying that prognosis would not stop me from finding a solution from among the many contacts with Nature Cure, herbalists and osteopath friends, and that in addition I would take him to see the London Spiritual Healer, Ted Fricker, whom I had met years before.

John responded very positively, his colour came back immediately and that was the start of the long road to Spiritual Healing.

There was no treatment under the NHS but Wilf Morley would do his best to get advice from all his NIMH (Member of the National Institute of Medical Herbalists).

As a result of the information he obtained he was able to prescribe a special medicine of herbs that would alleviate the symptoms and he would show me how to do a daily massage with special oils that would also help. It was late December 1966 – what a Christmas.

This was shattering news and we were all traumatised at first. Then we started on the new regime of herbs, oils and massage and John seemed to gather strength and courage. As he could no longer hold down a hard working job as a foreman at a large nursery in Shropshire we got him home and built a commercial size greenhouse in our field above the house. Then he rented a small shop in the village where he sold fruit, vegetables and flowers. Joyce helped in his business on flower arranging – particularly for funerals etc. and most important of all I decided to take him to see this wonderful healer Mr Fricker.

When we got to London he was not in attendance but a deputy treated John. The following business day I was telling a sympathetic customer about John and the trip to see Mr Fricker. The customer was well known in Sheffield and was Chairman of an important public company. He listened sympathetically and then surprised me by saying that he knew about Spiritual Healing; I did not need to go to London for one as there was a very good one in Sheffield. It was a Mr Ernest Webster, he was a spiritualist and medium and healer but I was not to tell anyone of my informant's interest as he 'was part of the Cathedral crowd'. I suppose he felt that it was somehow inconsistent with orthodox religion

So that started the long trail which lead the Bellinger family into Spiritual Healing and to a wider appreciation of the many spiritual gifts which were possible to discover among so many people. Because Ernest Webster was doing so much, so successfully, for John, it was natural that we should take an interest in the other pursuits that he was involved in. He was president of his particular Spiritualist Church; he was a medium and was clairvoyant, clairaudient, clairsentient. He could 'see' into the body (clairvoyantly) and tell what was wrong e.g. he could see into the kidneys and say if there were any stones there, say how many and in which kidney – and he would be right. His diagnosis was often confirmed by subsequent x-ray. He was able to converse with ones' loved ones who had died; tell you how and from what they had come to their life's end etc. He could always give some sign or proof that could not be doubted. Maybe these proofs were apparently trivial items, but because they were unknown to anyone else they could be very convincing, so John had his healing.

In 1970 John and Robert were both members of the Young Conservatives of the Hope Valley. They used to meet on a regular basis at one of our local Inns, and parents and others would be asked to speak to arouse their interest etc. John was Speaker-Finder and he had used up all the parent talent. I suggested that he should try Mr Webster who readily agreed. We felt that the usual Pub was not the right place for such a talk (Spiritualism) so they all came to our home; it was January 1970 I think.

John brought Ernest Webster as he did not have a vehicle and the gang arrived with Robert half an hour later.

When he arrived to be greeted by myself and Joyce he came into the house and exclaimed "What an atmosphere, it has not always been like this. You have brought it" and was visibly affected. It seemed that his face was being plucked from external sources. He came into the lounge and was introduced to my sister Connie. He said "You are in trouble my dear, you live in a big house where the lawn goes down to the river (correct); your husband is bad, he will leave you in August, and you will have to divorce him (all correct). He then said he could 'see' a previous owner of the house, said he had been in the Boer War (was showing the uniform) and his name was Brittlebank (proved to be correct). He later told Robert that he could be a healer, and a very good one. And three days later it had begun to manifest in aching hands etc. He was sitting on his hands, holding them under his armpits etc. I had just dislocated my right shoulder a few days earlier and it was proving very painful. He put his hands on my right shoulder at my request and something happened. Heat and energy radiated into my shoulder joint and peace was restored; all pain stopped.

He started to heal friends and family, various animals including dogs and horses. One example of the latter was the well known winner of many Flagg races owned by Peter

Sutherland. It was called Paradox and had developed problems. After treatment it won again, the farrier could not understand how the difference in condition had been caused; Paradox had already won the "Members" race 4 times in succession and after treatment went on to win twice more – a record which still stands.

The healing experience came to me about a year later. It happened like this: - I had got into the habit of treating John by massage every night at bed time. On this occasion John had been pricking out seedlings all day in his greenhouse and came down for tea saying his legs ached like toothache and could I possibly do the massage now instead of later. This I readily agreed and suggested that he should first have a hot bath and then I would anoint him with the rubbing oils and do the massage. After I had done about 30 minutes work on John's back and legs he said it felt no better, then Robert came in from his College of Surveyors. I asked him to give John healing to see if that would help. This he readily did; put down his satchel; held his hands about two feet above his back and let the flow occur. After about a minute or so John asked "Why are you digging your fingers in my back like that?" He turned his head and saw that there was no physical contact, relaxed and within moments he said that all the aches had disappeared. Robert then went over to his bed and started to get ready for the evening meal. I held my hands over John's back and said to myself "I wish I could do that" and lo and behold, John said "Why are you digging your fingers into my back?" and again he saw that there was no actual contact. I felt the flow of spiritual energy coming out of my fingers and I was quite overcome with emotion, elation, wonderment etc. I thought I might be getting the power from Robert who was still in the room, so we tried it the following night when Robert was not there and it happened in the same way again.

SO THAT WAS ME STARTED.

From then on I fulfilled my promise (to myself and Spirit) that I would use my gift to the benefit of all who asked for and needed healing. After about another year (again it was January), I felt rather drained after healing some twelve or so patients. I went into the dining room and asked Joyce if she would close her eyes and tell me if she could 'see' in the same way that Mr Webster could and so help me decide when to stop the healing. To my surprise she said that, like everybody, she could continue to see people when she had closed her eyes. She had assumed that it was normal and had never mentioned it to me or to her mother or friends. Apparently she saw people in colours i.e. the aura. She was able soon after to tell me what colours she actually saw and these indicated the condition of the patient and the stage of the healing process.

She could see my colour as, say, light blue whereas the patient would display various colours including dark muddy colours over part of his body; or violent red/black, dark grey or green. This always referred to the problem area from which they were suffering. As the process of healing progressed the patient would take on the same colour that I was showing. When it showed <u>all gold</u> we knew that the healing was complete for that time and/or that the condition was cured.

It was also realised that Joyce was herself giving healing and quite a number of patients would remark how powerful her healing was; they could feel the difference when she started. One particular patient (a very large fit fireman) would specifically ask for Joyce because he was aware of her power. We then noticed that Joyce would feel drained after giving healing – so we were careful not to let that happen in future. Another interesting gift that Joyce had was that she could 'see' the patients' loved ones who were with them during healing. She would describe them minutely; even draw their faces, when they were instantly recognised. She was a very good artist and liked portraiture. People were always surprised at the accuracy of her drawings or descriptions.

Over the following years we all became increasingly involved in Healing. Through the introduction of Ernest Webster, Joyce and I became members of the Essex County Healers Association of which Ernest was also a member. Some years later the NFSH (National Federation of Spiritual Healers), which had been founded by Harry Edwards and other leading healers, proposed that all members of the other county associations would be very welcome to transfer into the NFSH. It was to amalgamate and strengthen the movement and increase its influence.

This was largely successful and we transferred and became accredited healers of the National Federation of Spiritual Healers. This new body, with Harry Edwards as its chairman decided to organise the country into regions, and we became part of Region 9. The first area meeting took place while I was on holiday, so that I was unable to attend the first meeting of likely committee members, but one year later I attended the next committee AGM and was adopted as Chairman (Region 9). The secretary and I arranged several public demonstrations in such towns as Derby, Nottingham, Harrogate and Mansfield, all towns within the Region 9 area Derbyshire, Lincolnshire, South Yorkshire and North Nottinghamshire etc.

There were some good results obtained at these meetings where the members of the public formed an enthusiastic audience. The usual form was for the main Healer Demonstrator to be drawn from a known NFSH member and I would act as chairman of the meeting. On the occasion of the meeting in Nottingham it was held in the Albert Hall and the Healer was a Mr Tom Pilgrim with his helper a Mr Landon. After he had been introduced he asked if there was a case of anyone suffering from a cataract of the eyes. A young lady put up her hand and she was invited to the stage. She had a confirmed cataract of the right eye and Tom Pilgrim said, before we start will you please look at the clock, which was positioned over the entrance, and tell me the time. It was a large round clock with clear black figures. The patient looked and admitted that she could not see the clock. Tom then touched her forehead and she went 'to sleep' whilst still standing. Tom then went into trance and started speaking in German. He then made a few passes in front of her eye without touching her, and then came out of the trance and was caught, as he crumpled, by his colleague Lander who sat him on a chair. Tom stood up almost immediately and went to the patient and touched her forehead to wake her up. He then told her that she had had an operation and that she should not strain her eyes for 24 hours by reading or watching TV etc. But he then said "but before you go will you please tell us the time by the Hall clock" She looked at the clock and announced "It is twenty past three!"

In later contacts with this likeable healer he told me about an occasion that affected him which was very unusual. He apparently developed severe toothache and his local dentist discovered that the pain was caused by a very large abscess on his lower jaw. He alarmed him by saying that it would be necessary to break the jaw bone at that point. Tom said he could not accept such a solution and terminated the discussion. However, his doctor persuaded him that he ought to attend Guys Hospital where the experts would be able to help him without such drastic measures. When he was in the operating chair, with many student dentists watching this difficult case he suddenly went into trance, being taken over by his German Spirit doctor who told the professor dentist who was to conduct the operation, how he should carry out the procedure; what he would find and all the particular circumstances of the case.

Then Tom woke up and said he was sorry he had fallen asleep, as he thought he had. The dentist assured him that everything that his German doctor had said made absolute sense and he carried out the process with complete success, removed the abscess and laid it out in front of Tom's eyes. He told me it looked like a shining transparent slug. He was stitched up and allowed to go home. On his way to the exit, one of the other dental surgeons who had seen the operation and all that had happened, caught up with him and enquired where he could make further enquiries and study the wonderful Truths of Spirit and all about Spiritual Healing.

Tom and his companion were from the south coast not far from Brighton and they did a great deal of very good work – and all for free as was the case of most Federation healers.

Under the new organisation of the N.F.S.H. meetings were held every few months attended by the Chairman and Secretaries of all the 14 regions. I attended with Secretary Mrs Brown who lived in Nottingham.

At the first Annual General Meeting various reports were presented to the well attended meeting which was held in a hall at the London Festival Hall. When the treasurer gave his report I asked a few pertinent questions. When it came to the Election of Officers for the coming year they al asked if I would consent to nomination as Treasurer. I was pleased to accept nomination and was voted in unanimously.

I acted as treasurer for 3 years. Reorganised Bank Accounts and among other things exposed the then administrator's improper use of his authority and the Charities' funds. It led to his departure. The previous treasurer had been too trusting and this was revealed at a headquarter meeting when I was taking over! The administrator passed me the Charities cheque book to sign "in blank". That is what the previous treasurer had done. The administrator had only to apply his own signature to validate the payment. The board members were good healers no doubt, but very naïve trusting individuals.

I was amused on one occasion when the Head Quarters team met for a conference at the home of a healer member in a road not far from Piccadilly. It was her healing room that was to be used and it was below street level with glass bricks letting in light from the street above. In the alcove below the bricks was a small side table with a large blue and white serving dish with a large notice which said "For voluntary donations – minimum £5". (1980)

Spiritual Healing and Absent Spiritual Healing

I think it might be helpful if I explained a little about this wonderful Spiritual Healing; and Absent Healing. It has been described by Harry Edwards, who was one of the greatest Healers of modern times as follows:-

"Spiritual Healing is divine healing – that is, it comes from God and is His gift to all his children, regardless of race or creed. It is NOT Faith Healing. The term 'FAITH' infers that the success of the treatment depends on the implicit faith of the patient in the healer to overcome the trouble. If Spiritual Healing relied upon the faith of a patient for its results we should not see babies (who are incapable of expressing faith) respond to it. Nor would we see healing take place with those for whom help has been sought unbeknown to them, say by a friend or relative, nor for those whose minds are unbalanced".

I would add to that list and say that animals respond very well to healing and faith does not apply there either.

Generally, however, it is good for patients to have confidence in the power of Spirit to heal. Many patients come to us to try Spiritual Healing as a very last resort. They have tried orthodox medicine and other forms of treatment and when these have not succeeded they are prepared to 'risk it' and come to us. Very often there are surprising results. Some feel heat; some feel cold; some feel pressure and nearly all feel a great sense of peace and relaxation. Many drift off into a sleep state. And this will often last for as much as one hour. (See the case of Three Sleepy People from Leeds).

There has been plenty of evidence for many years that life continues after our so called 'death' and that it is possible for communication to occur between life on this earth and that from the realm of spirit.

For many people – patients in particular, the experience of having healing acts as a kind of catalyst and their minds become more open and ready to accept some of the truths of spirit. And we have seen many such instances aided by many gifted 'Mediums' who have spiritual gifts. Some have clairvoyance, clairaudience, clairsentience, etc. My wife, Joyce, could 'see' the aura and thereby tell where healing was needed. I found it helpful when treating patients. She could also 'see' patient's deceased loved ones; and could draw them and have recognition from the patient! They found that very convincing. The healer is a channel for the healing energies that are passed from our Spirit Doctors who can attune with the healer while the healer attunes to the patient.

Maxwell Cade used to work closely with the NFSH and carried out some experiments with 'Mind Mirrors' adapted to register the brain wave patterns (EEC's) of the Healer and a separate Mind Mirror on the patient; once attuned the two Mind Mirrors always showed the same reading. Similarly when Joyce was 'seeing' my aura while healing – my colours would be matched by those of the patient as soon as I had attuned and the healing was in progress.

Prophetic Dreams

Throughout my life, from childhood to adult life, I have experienced dreams which were sufficiently impressed upon my mind that I remembered them fully on waking. Many were so exact in their facts that it was quite uncanny. One example occurred when I was only about seven or eight years of age, when I was still recovering from the illness I have previously mentioned, T.B.

In this dream I saw an oaken short stave suddenly sprout wings and fly over a strange country. It was about two feet eight inches long and the thickness of a stout walking stick. When I told my mother what I had dreamt she said, "I know what that means. You are going to travel to the Holy Land and see all the special places that were important to Jesus of Nazareth". This came true twenty years later in the war years when I was drafted to Palestine with the 1st Cavalry division as a trooper in the Yorkshire Dragoons. I had joined the 'A' Squadron in Sheffield in 1938 when the war seemed inevitable.

After we had been in Palestine a few months the regiment was stationed at the foot of the Mount of Sacrifice which to me loomed very large in the Bible. I climbed this mountain several times and on the crest was a monastery. The monks there were very friendly to me; gave me refreshments and on the final visit; they told me I would not be there again and they would like me to have a memento of my visits; gave me – you've guessed it – an oaken stave which had been taken from the stunted oak trees that grew on the side of the mountain. They offered me one of two, and I chose the shorter one 2' 8" in length (as it would fit in my kit bag) and I carried it with me throughout my service in the Middle East, and I have it still.

Another dream occurred when I was commissioned into the RAPC and was stationed in York. It was while there that I had married and we had been able to rent a furnished house on the outskirts of York for about £2.00 per week. In a dream an old lady came to me and told me that my wife was pregnant; that it would be a boy and that all would be well. The lady in the dream was Joyce's grandmother who was Welsh and whose photograph I saw later, exactly as she had appeared to me. John was born on the 8th June 1943.

Another dream occurred when I and my family were on holiday in the Western Highlands. We were camping in the region of Loch Torridon, near Badachro. I remember that we had pitched our tent on a sward of bluebells which could not be avoided. I had dreamt this dream over three successive nights. In the dream I was back in the Army and the two senior officers who appeared were in fact the District Manager and the Chairman of the Board of Local Directors who controlled the Branch bank (very small of which I was manager). In the dream I had to report to the Major (District Manager) who told me that they were thinking of promoting me to full majority (i.e. to Major from my present rank of Captain). He told me there were other possible candidates but the Colonel would let me know soon. The following night the same scene appeared and this time I also saw the Colonel, who confirmed he was thinking of promoting me but that Brigade Head Quarters might also have a candidate. The third night I was back again and this time the Colonel told me that their minds were made up and I would be their choice provided that Head Quarters did not insist on having their own choice.

When I returned to my branch after the holiday my senior clerk told me that Local Head Quarters had been asking for me, not being reachable by phone because I was camping, they had had to await my return; and I was to attend at Local Head Office, Nottingham as soon as possible. When I arrived the District Manager and the Local Chairman of Directors all said what they had said in the dream. I eventually got the promotion and it was to the main branch in Derby where they had a major branch with an appointed chief clerk.

There was another interesting matter that was involved in this dream. Some years before when I was acting as Chief clerk in the Local Head Office in Sheffield I had had to carry out an A.D.C type duty on the occasion of an official visit from the Staff General Manager. He was called Mr Boyd. I had met him at the Sheffield Midland Railway Station. Complete with my small car with the purpose of taking him to various branches in our area so that he could see and interview possible subjects for promotion.

When he came out of the station approach I was able to recognise him from photographs I had seen. He was wearing a somewhat tatty reversible raincoat/cum tweed effect. The hem was hanging down in several places; his shoes were not clean; his trilby hat looked as though he had used it to clean his car. I was very surprised that a man in his position could turn out in such a dishevelled state. Naturally I did not say anything to him or anyone else.

Having told me that I was to be their choice for promotion, the local DTR told me that I would have to attend shortly at Head Office in London; that I would be interviewed by various General Managers and one of these would be a Mr BOYD. He told me that from his conversations with Mr Boyd that he had an inferiority complex where I was concerned and he told me to make it easy for him to interview me. He must have got thought transference from me when I met him at the station all that time ago. I certainly thought that if I were General Manager I would not turn out like that when representing the Bank.

Another example occurred in the late 1960's and on a more material level. It was like this: - over a few years I had been buying shares in a company which banked with my Sheffield branch. It was a company based in Sheffield and its main board directors were well known to me and one, the chairman, was a friend of long standing. These shares had started at only 7 pence each and I had acquired a few thousand. Other friends had also followed my lead and they too had in total several more thousand shares. In my dream I heard a voice say "Sell your ..... shares. You will get 18 pence each for them". When I got to the office and put in an enquiry the brokers quoted 19.5 pence. So I asked my friends if they also wanted to sell and they all said "Yes". When I put in the order to sell I duly got 18 pence as the dream voice had said!

There have been several similar dreams in which I have been told the result of healing cases long before the eventual 'passing' or complete cure.

One such case involved a boy of 3½ years who came in March 1999 with brain stem cancer and no prospect of living more than a few weeks. In six months he went back to school. However, he had become infected with some sort of virus after swimming in a public pool much against my advice! It started in his ears, transferred to his sinuses and finally his chest. This developed into pneumonia and he sadly died some nine or ten months after first coming to us. The chemotherapy and radiation destroys the normal immunity and the patient is open to every infection. The dream came to me in late April after about six weeks into his treatment. I dreamt that the telephone rang and when I answered it. It was the boy's father telling me with sobs in his voice that his son had just died. I made a note in my diary but told no-one, hoping it would not become fact. Sadly it did.

This power to transmit thought was of great use in a later case which is detailed under the name of Kenneth Wilson among the Case Histories.

Sheffield

In 1965 the Bank promoted me to be manager of the main Sheffield Branch which was sited in Fitzalan Square, on the corner of Commercial Street. It was planned to replace these premises with a new building, the plans for which were already completed – so I had no influence on design. However, I had worked at this same branch before the war and also immediately after the war, under a Mr Chamberlain, so many of the circumstances and customers were known to me. It was to be a prestige branch with first floor banking hall, escalators, caretaker's apartment on the top floor, special board room for important conferences and entertaining, and several lifts. There was also to be a separate strong room for the purpose of a central reserve facility for the other branches of the area. The various hall staircases were to be marble lined and the three rooms for management were to look out on to a cut off decorative area with a small fountain, artificial frogs etc. again all in marble.

The main banking hall was to have provision for under floor heating in the customer section and the main central heating was to be overhead. (So we could have hot heads and cold feet unless you stayed in the banking hall area).

The branch was also to have extensive car parking in a basement underneath and a separate area for staff and service vehicles which came out on to a lower road. In addition to the customer car park there was a separate floor above the car park which provided approach to the special strong room for the central reserve or for vehicles which collected or delivered bullion. This floor was also provided with a large turntable to enable these vans to be turned round; and this area was protected with a very strong portcullis for controlling admissions etc.

This building work went on apace and took very little of my time as it was all controlled through Premises Dept Head Office. The appointed architects were a London based firm called Lloyds. The Mr Lloyd that was in charge of the project was a very tall lean man and he would come to make his inspections on a regular basis. As it neared completion I felt I should invite him to take lunch with me and he accepted my invitation to meet at the Grand Hotel in the town centre. I reserved a table and he arrived on time only to reject the thought of eating a meal – he only had a drink at lunch time. So I had to cancel the table and took him to the cocktail bar and ordered a tray of fresh sandwiches. He then drank several large gin and tonics but ate none of the food. I then took him to the new building and left him to do his inspections.

The following day his wife rang me to tell me off for letting her husband get drunk. He had arrived home with a very small overcoat which he had mistakenly taken from the hotel as we left. So I had to explain that he had full responsibility for all that had happened and I had been unable to persuade him to have a normal lunch. I also got back his overcoat and apologised to the hotel and its other customers for the mix up of coats.

There was one further funny incident with this Mr Lloyd. On completion and at the ceremony, we had a big party for customers and for all top men of the contractors Henry Boot.

My Local Directors had asked me to reserve a private room at the Grosvenor Hotel to give a meal to all the V..IP.'s in addition to drinks and refreshments at the Bank. We came to the end of the meal and then David Traill (Chairman of the Local Head Office) made a valedictory little speech. He finished by inviting Mr Lloyd to respond. Lloyd rose slowly to his full height without a single word, and then passed out and fell right across the table – blind drunk. Mr Traill asked me to take appropriate action. Which I did!!

I then returned to the branch to see the end of that party at which I had had to leave my wife, Joyce. She had had many attempts to sip champagne but on each try she had been interrupted, had put down her glass and found it had been removed by waiters as she came back to claim it. Several staff members were slightly the worse for drink and an insurance agent was seen feeling his way along the wall trying to find the exit.

The catering had been expertly provided by Sante Perez of the Red Lion at Standedge. The final bill included 150 bottles of vintage champagne (Dom Perignon). This same hotel – owned by a customer, was where we held my son Robert's 21st birthday party. Sante Perez was a wonderful chef and had been a top Barcelona footballer. He once had a luncheon booking for a special party for the Duchess of Devonshire. A few days before the event he had a visit from one of the Ladies in Waiting who wanted to check that the 'Arrangements' were in order. He invited her into his office and referred to his notes. She said "You don't understand – I have come to see all the 'Arrangements' are satisfactory. So Sante said "What do you mean then?" She replied "I have come to check that the toilets are acceptable". They were!

I decided that it would be a very good idea to try out the facilities for entertaining in "the Banks" beautiful Board Room. For safety I also decided that the first run would be for members of my staff and the other branch managers from the Sheffield area. So invitations were issued and the Caretakers wife was consulted and confirmed that she would be able to cook the lunch, the food for which I would be responsible.

So I bought a joint of meat, sprouts, potatoes, carrots etc. and timed the meal to start at one o'clock preceded by cocktails. I had already bought the best quality china (Crown Derby) and the best quality cutlery and carving set and felt confident as to the outcome. It was just as well I had decided to have a test run. The meat was so tender that I could not cut a slice without the meat crumbling into a gentle heap. The sprouts were a soggy mess and so it went on. I came back to the office and asked my secretary, Miss Kate Belk, to go up and sort out what had happened. She came back eventually with a big smile on her face. She had been able to fathom what had gone wrong. Apparently the Caretaker's wife had to cook all her husband's food until it was 'mushy' because he ate his meals without his dentures. No wonder we had such a problem. She had asked Miss Belk what she should do with the overcooked sprouts. Miss Belk took a look at them and said "Sling them". In all future occasions I gave the 'Cook' careful instructions as to how to cook everything and we had no further problems.

There were sub-branches under my control; at Eckington;

Attercliffe; Bannercross and Woodseats. The Eckington Branch catered for this mining village and at this time it was manned by Harry Manning, who had come to us from Chief Foreign Branch when it was shedding surplus staff. He would come back with some interesting stories. One concerned a housewife from there who had received some newspaper publicity. This was because she had just given birth to her twentieth child. The ladies of Sheffield W. I. saw this as an opportunity to get a little publicity in support of women's lib. They formed a group to act as a deputation to call on her and offer their commiserations. Dressed in their smartest they duly called at the lady's house and she received them standing at her front door which was a few steps above the pavement. She listened to their statement and how they were so disgusted that she had been made to have so many children etc. She then told them they were wasting their time; she had enjoyed having the children and was only sorry she could not now have any more. She told them that as each new babe arrived she had left it to the older children to bring up and she had bought a new puppy to match the baby and they all went under the table in the kitchen. She closed the interview telling them they could all **** off

The Attercliffe branch was quite near to the industrial side of Sheffield and there was a high proportion of Indian and Pakistani residents and workers. When the bank introduced the 'Barclay Loan' the clerk in charge came to me with the request that I should see the leader of these workers. He came to me and said that he liked the idea of the new loan which could amount to as much as £500 and for any purpose; repayments were to be monthly and there was no need for security. He said that he would be prepared to give me a personal guarantee that any borrower that he introduced would honour his commitment. So I agreed and we had a very good run on this scheme. Once or twice we told him of a backslider and in each case the culprit was walked into the branch with this leader close behind him – with a concealed knife pressed against his ribs. We had no Bad Debts in this department at this branch!

However, we did experience a strange case with a loan taker where the husband died during the course of the repayment and where he had not availed himself of the optional insurance policy. I asked the security clerk to call on the widow to ascertain the facts. He came back and told me the widow had several children; her income had suddenly halved with her husband's death, the Roman Catholic priest was still calling for his contribution which he absolutely insisted on collecting. So I decided to write to the Roman Catholic Bishop of Sheffield to inform him of this hardship. In his very brief reply he said he had told the local priest to hold back on his collecting until the Bank Loan was fully repaid and that he would then resume his normal collections!

The banking hall was approached from the ground floor by escalator, one for up and one for down. In the opening week we saw a very large and much overweight black lady try to get up on the 'down' escalator – she persisted most nobly and finally succeeded – completely out of breath.

Another unexpected effect was caused by the tinkling visible fountain in the display area of the management rooms. Elderly men who saw it were inclined to need to find a toilet – I don't think the architects had anticipated that one.

Towards the end of my service with the bank I was elected President of the Sheffield Institute of Bankers and had many official functions to attend. In addition to the normal 12 months of duty I had to do an extra three months because the previous President got promoted to a far off area and so I had to step into his shoes and add these extra three months. In this 15 months of duty I attended 110 luncheons/dinners and gatherings. I had to drive myself and take full part throughout. I am happy to report that my weight was the same at the end as at the beginning – and I am still the same after 30 years of retirement.

The other major branch was in the High Street and above this office was the old Local Head Office suite of offices. When this branch lost its manager, Alec Neill, through retirement, the new manager was the ex L.H.O. manager, Peter Stevenson. He told me later that the Local Directors had instructed him to find a house within the Sheffield area. **They did not want another country squire (like me!)**

David Traill had his retirement party at a hotel in central Nottingham. All managers were guests at the dinner. On the completion of the meal David made a farewell speech thanking us all for our efforts and loyalties. When he finished Ken Murgattroyd of Gallowtree Gate, Leicester Branch (our biggest) responded suitably. He sat down to the cheers of his audience; he then keeled over and died. Gar Grey who had been his predecessor had only lived 12 months or so in his retirement when he too had dropped dead in his bathroom; another statistic towards the assessment of only one and a quarter years of enjoyment of pension of Barclay Managers (when retirement age only 60). This is what I had been told by a colleague who worked in Staff Dept. and was a strong argument in favour of keeping fit; controlling stress levels; being abstemious with drinks and cigarettes etc.

Throughout the whole of my time in the Derby Office and in Sheffield, Fitzalan Square, I had a great deal of pleasure in the game of golf. While in Derby I became the area golf secretary for the various Spring, Summer and Autumn meetings. These were open to area teams and also to individual entries and were arranged at famous internationally known golf courses.

Those in Scotland included St Andrews – the home of golf; Troon; Turnberry and others. In England there was Aldburgh; St Georges; Jersey; a course near Cardiff and Aston near Birmingham. They were all three day events and all at the banks expense – so it was like an extra holiday. If wives went then that expense was bourne by each individual.

Our L.H.O. Chairman, Mr David Traill was a keen golfer and usually attended at the personal level; I often played with or against him in these various matches. I was lucky enough to win the BRYAN Trophy in the Summer meeting about 1965/1966, this was for the second class handicaps (14 to 18) and I was able to return a net 68. In later years I achieved wins in the Veteran class. I also won the Local Directors Cup for the Nottingham L.H.O. Area twice: the Veterans class here also and also for the Veterans Cup in the later Summer meetings. It usually turned out that my putting had been better than usual and I had managed to produce something like 9 to 11 single puts. When I played St Andrews with David Traill in a match I achieved three holes in two. It was at this match that the Secretary of the British Linen Bank, who was doing some early morning practice with me said that he had heard from David Traill that I was the manager with the biggest Housing Loan in the L.H.O area.

Long after we had both retired when Joyce and I were taking a caravan holiday in Aberlady (where David had gone to live) that I met him quite by chance in the Aberlady Health Food Store. He was dressed in Plus-Fours and was burdened with shopping bags. After greeting me he said, "You were always a very good putter, what was your system? Do please tell me." So looking very serious I told him that I relied on my first assessment of the line and strength, then closed my eyes, and made the stroke. I don't know whether he really believed me! Then he asked if I still lived in that little country cottage in Hathersage. I said "Yes", but did not tell him how the valuation had soared. It might have increased his blood pressure. Shortly after this meeting he had a severe stroke and did not survive very long.

In Doncaster, Derby and Sheffield I was a member of the Round Table – later to become a member of the 41 Club. I played in their golf competition and twice won the Wilkinson Sword Dagger in the Sheffield match.

Gordon Higginson

Gordon Higginson was a brilliant medium: his mother was a fine medium and trained him from childhood in the many skills of mediumship.

When we first met him he was giving a demonstration of his gifts at the Sheffield Psychical Research Society. He was President of the Spiritual National Union and also of his local Spiritualist Church in Longton, near Stoke-on-Trent; he obviously thought a lot of Mavis Pittilla and had no doubt contributed to her development as a medium. We attended a series of long weekend seminars, first at Lytham St Anne's and thereafter at Ruthin Castle Hotel in Ruthin, North Wales: $3^{rd} - 6^{th}$ November 1989, $2^{nd} - 5^{th}$ November 1990 and $1^{st} - 4^{th}$ November 1991.

It was at the Lytham meeting that my patient Betty Waterall had her experience of his mastery of mediumship (see separate case history).

Once at the Ruthin seminar I asked Jean McIntyre, his secretary, if she would book a reading for the two of us with Gordon.. She said "He never sees husband and wife together – he sees too much of their secrets". I replied we had none and would she please ask him. This she did and to her evident surprise he had accepted our "together" reading.

When we entered his room he said he would start on Joyce and asked for something from her handbag to hold and make the contact. Joyce produced a purse or glasses case and he went into his reading. He started off by saying we had three children – Joyce said, "only two". He said but you had a miscarriage, it was to have been a girl – a long pause – and then "goodness me she is now your grand-daughter Chalene. I have never known such a quick reincarnation".

Then he said "Why, oh why did your younger son marry THAT GIRL. They are worlds apart". He will come back to live in your house in a few years time". Correct.

Then he told me about my healing and that it would go on to the end of my life. In fact he said "You will be healing as you are dying".

Another story was about his mother. When she became old and housebound she expressed a wish for some new glasses. So Gordon asked an optician to call with his samples. She rejected his samples saying she wanted some like Dame Edna Everidge. These eventually arrived but she died before anyone had seen her wearing them.

Then at a time when he was giving a three day lecture in Birmingham University on the paranormal, he was approached by a young lady who said she would like to sit in on his lecture, although she wasn't a university student, as she would like to do psychic drawings of her impressions during his talk. This he readily agreed to. At the end of the programme he asked her how she had got on. She surprised him by saying that she had been "forced to do a drawing by unknown influences". Gordon asked to see it. It was a portrait of his mother and she was wearing the Dame Edna spectacles. The artist then got up and just disappeared.

There was also a strange incident at Stansted Hall which was the H.Q. of the SNU. This was many years ago when the previous president had just passed to spirit and he had been asked to attend at Stansted. This hall had been left to the SNU by a successful Glasgow stockbroker, J Arthur Findlay; author of a wonderful trilogy on spiritualism which I recommend everyone should read. When he arrived at the Hall the administrator said there was a monk waiting to see him and he was shown into the library to be greeted by the monk. He said his organisation knew of Gordon and his gifts and wanted him to accept the Presidents position. He pressed Gordon to accept with many cogent arguments. Gordon said he would like a short time and chance to talk it over with the administrator. So he went out of the library, had his discussion outside the library door and finally agreed to the appointment. He went back into the library and the monk was not there: and no other door!

The day that Joyce Bellinger passed to Spirit

It was on Wednesday the 24th November 1999; and this is a brief summary of the events as they occurred on that memorable, sad day.

First thing that morning I awoke at about 6 a.m. to find that Joyce was not in bed. I thought that she might be in the bathroom and might be needing help. So I went to see. She was not in the bathroom but I saw that the kitchen light was on and so I went downstairs and found her well advanced in preparations for making our Christmas cakes; mixing fruit etc. So I said that that could wait and that she could leave it to me to finish and that she should go back to bed. I helped her up the stairs and back into bed and then used the bathroom myself to shave and bathe. When I went back into the bedroom Joyce was asleep in her reclining position which helped her breathing.

So I then went downstairs and prepared breakfast; I had mine, and then took up a tray for Joyce. It was tea, toast, half a grapefruit etc. When I went back to see how she was getting on I found that she had eaten the grapefruit and had had one cup of tea but she did not want anything else. By this time it was about 9 a.m. and I asked her what she would like to do. Get up and go for a drive in the car? Go for a short walk around the garden? Go shopping? The answer was 'no', none of those things. 'Had I rung Robert?' (This we often did at 9.15 a.m. when we could be sure of getting him alone). To this I replied that I had not tried as I knew that Robert had an appointment in London for that morning at 10 a.m. and he would have left home by 7.30 a.m. (Sadly he had cancelled that appointment on a premonition so we could have in fact spoken).

Joyce then said that she felt so very peaceful that she would just like to stay in bed and talk, and asked me to sit on the bed beside her and just talk. So this is what we did. After a few minutes of idle chatter, I started doing my neck and eye exercises and Joyce remarked that at my age I should cut out some of my energetic activities and learn to slow down. To this I replied that I could not stop now; I'd done it all my life and one day I wanted to be the fittest corpse in the mortuary.

At this she laughed – then gasped; and she was gone. I realised what had happened and tried to resuscitate her but it had no effect. Then I rang for the doctor (David Moseley); then Robert, who said he would come immediately. The doctor came and said that it was a sudden death, he would have to notify the police and there would have to be a post mortem. He explained that even though the death had been forecast by him some eight months or so before, he had not actually seen Joyce for more than fourteen days and that was now the law.

So the police came very shortly after and asked me a lot of questions and finally took Joyce's body to the Coroner's in Buxton; and they carried out the P.M. and released the body a few days later to the undertaker Ted Noutch of the Hope Valley.

From that day onwards there were lots of paranormal manifestations and I have decided for the benefit of any interested party I have made the following list of the more obvious ones:-

- When Robert arrived from his home in West Sussex he said that he would take me out for a meal to our friendly local, and this we did. We came home to have coffee. When this was made, I took Joyce's favourite white chocolate 'After Eight' dinner mints to have with our coffee. When I opened the box I found there were only two left each in its own gold wrapping envelope. So we each had one. When we finally went off to bed at about 1.30 a.m. I took the empty box, turned it upside down and showed it to Robert as being empty. Then I closed the lid and placed the box in the 'Jotul' stove on top of the unlit coals. In the morning when I came to open the curtains my eyes were constantly drawn to this box of Dinner Mints. So I lifted it out of the stove and turned it over to see if the base was soiled by contact with the coal. To my surprise and disbelief I felt and heard something inside. When I opened the box **it was to find two more mints inside complete with their gold envelopes. (So we ate them). The next night we again put the empty box in the stove – but it was still empty the following morning!**
- Gladys Powell, a friend in the village who has mediumistic gifts heard Joyce's voice say "Tell Alan his black tie is in the wardrobe".
- Janet Fell heard Joyce say 'Lilies of the Valley' at 12.30 and at 4.30 woke up to the scent of Joyce's face cream.
- Friday night 1.30 a.m. Saturday morning, Tricia Hhusband was making a last cup of tea, having been out to a late dinner party, when she told her mother later that day that she had seen Joyce Bellinger walk

through her kitchen 'and I wasn't frightened mummy' she said. A few days later, she and her husband Thomas were again in the kitchen, this time Joyce had come to her and patted her on the shoulder and told her she would be alright. (It happened that Tricia had been having disturbing sensations and was to consult a specialist). Joyce was right, the symptoms were not of a life threatening nature, and it was Raynauds disease. Finally, Tricia and party were out walking when Joyce caught up with her and put her hand on her shoulder; this time Tricia reacted sharply and asked to be left alone. Since then she has not seen her.

- This sighting was by John Cattell who saw Joyce driving a car along Abbeydale Road. (Joyce does not and cannot drive).

- Mary Gains, a long time friend and hairdresser who lived fairly nearby, carried out her normal Friday change of bed linen. When she actually came to bed that night she turned down the coverlet in order to get into bed and there in the middle of her bed space was one of Joyce's very individual tortoise shell decorative hair pins. Mary never had any of these and only applied the ones supplied by Joyce.

- Robert was telling his friend Michael Foljambe about Joyce's activities and he surprised Robert by asking if he wanted to know where Joyce had been on the Sunday night. Yes said Robert 'with Gwen all Sunday night ' was the reply, Gwen was Miss Theaker who had been Michael's housekeeper until ill health had led to her retirement. (She and Joyce were very friendly. Gwen had been very kind and helpful to Robert).

- On Wednesday the 1st December 1999 Justin Fellowes was driving over Burbage Moors to come and see us when he saw a very wonderful display of colours in the sky above our house. It was midday and a column of rainbow colours was rising and falling from the ground into the clouds. He was thinking of Joyce when he saw this (this young man had been very close to us after we had been involved in the healing of his little boy).

- I woke up very early one morning and as I settled down to go back to sleep I suddenly felt that I was in a different place. There were trees in the background and I was sitting at the foot of a slight grassy bank. Joyce appeared suddenly and slid down the bank towards me. She was smiling happily saying 'I was so glad to find I wasn't dead'.

And there were many more incidents from mutual friends – and she had also been seen by patients including 'Nelson'.

- Joseph Hill, a long time patient reported in March 2000 that he had a stone in his kidney and that it was causing him great discomfort, even sharp pains. I gave him healing for this when he brought Nelson Dethick, his nearly blind friend (Nelson's son was married to Joe's daughter). While treating Nelson he always 'goes off' into a sort of deep sleep, during which Joyce would see him talking with his parents and grandparents among others. On this occasion when he woke up, he said that Joyce had been to see him and had given him the message that Joe's kidney stone would be dissolved by my treatment. When they came back the following week Joe reported that in the two days that followed his treatment all the pain had gone. Then the doctor's X-ray had shown that the stone was no longer there.

- Yesterday, the 27th June 2001, Joe brought Nelson after a period of several weeks of not being allowed to come because of the foot and mouth epidemic. As I began to treat Nelson I asked mentally for Joyce to visit him and leave me a message. He slept for 50 minutes and woke up to say how wonderful it had been. When asked, he had to disappoint me that Joyce had not been to see him. I was sorry. Then the following morning the 28th June the telephone rang before 8 a.m. and it was Justin Fellowes (whose son we had treated) to say that he and his wife had had a message from Joyce the previous night. They had been 'sitting' trying to communicate with their son, Connor, when Joyce made herself known. She said that Alan had wanted a message, please tell him that she had been with me in the garden (I had been cutting the lawns etc.) and wanted me to know that she had been with me and given me a hug and kisses. How remarkable. I do wish she had come direct; but what very good proof.

- Ingrid Bellfield, a psychic artist we met unexpectedly in February/March 2000 at the home of another healer/medium who was known to Justin Fellowes, he had taken Robert and me to their healing sanctuary to join in their healing efforts. Ingrid had arrived a little later to tell us that she had known she was to meet us and had had a visit from Joyce who had been in a very happy state; she had inspired her to draw two portraits, one for me and one for Robert. Mine she said was a picture of 'my other woman'; I said that I never had had another woman. I finally remembered that it was a very good likeness of the chaperone older girl who had been guarding Joyce the first time we had met! I have old snaps that prove the likeness.

A FEW INTERESTING CASES

The case of the Chihauhua in El Portet, near Moraira, Spain

Joyce and I were guests of our friends, Kit and Peter Nicol, at their villa near this lovely sandy bay with hills rising at either end of the bay. Having walked along the beach we walked up the pathway to the headland to the west of the bay. From this eminence we looked back and saw a local woman carrying a small dog, I think it was a chihauhau, then she walked into the sea until the water was up to her thighs, then she lowered the dog into the sea and let go of it. She continued looking out to sea, but the dog immediately turned round and started swimming for the shore. Ignoring the dog the old lady still looked out to sea. She appeared to be praying and crossed herself in the way Roman Catholics do. The dog by then had reached the shallow water which was still subject to rippling tiny waves.

It was only then that I saw that the dog was very restricted in that it could only use its front legs and it was attempting to drag itself from the sea and up the beach. At this point we turned back down the hillside to return to the beach to try and help. Before we lost sight of the dog we saw another Spanish man walk to the dog and drag it clear of the water. He then walked away as though he had done his bit. When we got to the scene the man had disappeared, and the woman had begun to come back to the shore. I told Joyce that I would give the dog healing for its paralysed back legs and walked to where it was spread-eagled on the wet sand. I held my hands over the sad little animal until the flow of healing had stopped, and then walked backwards to leave some space around the dog while being able to observe results, if any. To our delight instead of the dog scrabbling with its front legs only, it suddenly stood up on all four legs; shook itself vigorously and trotted off up the beach to where there were some houses.

By this time the woman had come close to me; she crossed herself and said some words in Spanish which I assumed to mean 'Thank you' and then made rapid tracks to follow the dog. The dog had obviously made an almost miraculous recovery.

The case of Mrs Amos and later her friend Mrs Hall (May 1977)

Ruth Amos came for healing while I was still working part-time as a financial consultant. She was suffering from a trapped nerve in the neck, shoulder and arm. She responded immediately and was OK. She told me she had had 'visions' after the healing and went off to Norfolk for a holiday to get away from problems with her husband, she saw more visions.

She came often over the following years with family problems with daughter, grandson etc. but in 1978. She called me to help with a Mrs Hall, who had M.S.; she had been a school headmistress, and Ruth was attending at her home to give general help.

Mrs Hall could not speak, but could write, and after several visits asked me to write out the spiritual philosophy behind the healing. This I did and she thanked me. Some time later Joyce rang me to say would I call at her home on my way from work in Chapeltown, as she was very ill and all her relatives were gathering. This was on a Wednesday morning and I duly gave her healing. She died on the following Saturday.

On the Monday following, Ruth attended for a 'reading' from a medium, a Mrs Wilkinson, whose skills I had recommended to Ruth. Mrs Wilkinson told Ruth the various facts that she wanted and then said that Mrs Hall had <u>danced</u> into their presence; she wanted to thank Ruth for the help and care she had given, and would she give Mr Bellinger a message please? The message was that though he had wonderful healing hands, he had not been able to heal her body but <u>he had healed her soul</u>, and for that she was very, very grateful. She had had trouble in her marriage apparently; her husband had gone off with his secretary and left her with her illness! The great stress had no doubt had its effect and helped cause the M.S.

I still get the occasional call or visit from Ruth and always get a card at Christmas.

Letter of Acknowledgement

To Mr & Mrs Bellinger & family

With my grateful thanks for having been brought into contact with you wonderful people.
Without your friendship my life would be empty, but you have given me life which is becoming more beautiful and understanding every day.
Sincerely,
Ruth Amos.

The case of Professor Steve Billings (18.04.85)

Stephen came to us as an introduction from Duncan Kitchen who did some work at the Sheffield University; (I think he was a psychologist). He had had surgery for testicular cancer and the secondaries appeared, just before we met him, in his lymphatic system. He was on chemotherapy and had had radiotherapy after the first operation. He was highly sensitive, intelligent and had lots of drive. He had been running businesses for members of his family and also for himself; and I think it had proved exciting but stressful

He responded very well to our healing but could very well panic tremendously at the finding of fresh 'lumps' in neck, groin or wherever. When this happened he would come especially at short notice and have some more healing – to which he always responded very well.

The 23rd of September 1985 came with news of a fresh nodule in the base of his neck. His pulse was taken at 180! His wife came from a family of doctors and was unhappy at the way we suggested he should avoid further surgery. He agreed to come for three more weekly healings. On 10th of October 1985 he had a scan performed and was very worried as to the findings. Joyce could see the aura colours in gold around the throat and said that it was therefore OK and Steve agreed to come weekly for a further period of six weeks. On 17th October 1985 we had a phone call from Steve. He was very excited and overjoyed – the scan was clear. On 4th of April 1986, reported still clear.

We had told him how to do 'meditation and visualization' and that he should take steps to reduce his stress factors, and this he had done. So he told us that he had made arrangements to take his family on holiday to Wales. The day before he was due to go he called on us in absolute panic state to say he had found another lump at the base of his neck. We treated him and Joyce could 'see' that it was not cancer. So we told him that he should still go on holiday and that perhaps the lump was there for a perfectly simple reason; such as draining some excess toxicity etc. So, off he went, calm again. About a week later we got a postcard from him from Wales which said 'Hooray, I've only got measles'.

He still calls to see us at least once a year just to let us see how very well he is keeping. He gets to his University office very early and then only works till midday, then recreation. He's fine and clear of cancer.

The case of Pauline Brown (friend of Fay Plant)

Pauline came to us first in February 1984. She had been the victim of a house burglar who had beaten her and left her with damage to her kidneys. When she came to our notice she had had an operation for cancer, I believe of the bowel. She was a wealthy lady and had the finest surgeons to do the operation. Then we were told by our friend Fay that she had developed cancerous fibroids in the uterus; would we do absent healing for her? This we did and she was again operated on by her surgeons. To their surprise they found that the five fibroids of 7½ and 5½inches and smaller (five in all) were detached and in plastic like sacs which were removed quite easily. They even communicated with their top colleague who was in Hong Kong to come and see the remarkable specimens.

In December 1985, five more growths were found attached to her pelvis. More absent healing was given. Later in the month she had an operation to remove them and to her joy they were found to be non-malignant.

In January 1988 she rang to tell us that she had had a precautionary scan and had been given an 'all-clear' verdict. They also told her that she was the only one of her original ward of cancer patients who was still alive, and also 'clear'. In April 1992 we were again asked to do absent healing as she had cancer in the upper vagina. On 11th May we were told there had been an outpouring of pus etc. to a total weight of 7lbs. In November that same year we were told that she was out dancing again and in March 1993 told that a fresh scan had again resulted in an 'all clear'.

After a few more alarms and absent healings in March 1994 we heard that there had been some heavy discharge but that it had been drainage from an abscess and not cancer. Her professor had apparently asked to see me – but that was never arranged. She finally died in September 1994 while Fay, Joyce and I were on holiday in Scotland. It was while we were having dinner in the Marine Hotel, North Berwick that we were suddenly very aware of the scent of freesias – her favourite flowers. Fay later was able to confirm that that was when she died.

Throughout the whole time we had been treating her she had been able to enjoy life very fully – dancing, partying, exotic holidays, shopping etc. She always looked like a beautiful doll to the very end. She had lots of stress from difficulties in her marriage and from problems with her children. I'm sure it had a great deal to blame for her difficult health problems.

The case of Tricia Caplan and kidney problems in the early 1970's

Joyce and I were invited to dinner by Mrs Gladys Caplan at their home in Dore Road Sheffield. The door was opened by their younger daughter, Tricia; when asked how she was, she said that apart from the trouble with her kidneys she was alright. She went on to say that she felt great pain in the kidneys and that she had to take painkillers every two hours or so as otherwise it was too painful to bear. So I said 'Aren't you lucky, we can treat that' and having made our "Hello's" to the mother and her elder sister Stephanie we started to give Tricia healing. Joyce was already able to 'see' and she stood behind Tricia while I positioned myself in front of her. I felt the flow of healing energies directed towards the kidneys, while Joyce reported that she could see a black band across the middle of about three inches in depth. As the healing progressed Joyce reported that she could see little flashes of light blue darting into the black areas until it was all blue and the black had disappeared. So I said that was 'it' and that now she was better. Joyce told me later that while we were doing the healing she could see the spirit of the recently deceased father (Maurice) sitting in his usual armchair. Although Joyce had not met Maurice when he was alive, her description was perfect.

We then had a very lively and enjoyable meal which must have lasted about two hours. Tricia suddenly spoke up and said, 'If I had not had your healing I would have been screaming for a painkiller by now'. She never had any further pain or trouble with her kidneys. However some time in the next year or so we were told by Mrs Caplan that Tricia was very ill with meningitis. Would we please be good enough to treat her for that? So I went to see her and duly gave her the healing. She got better with no further trouble.

When Joyce died one Wednesday morning, Tricia rang her mother on the next Saturday morning to tell her that Joyce Bellinger had walked through her kitchen while she was making a late night drink and 'I wasn't frightened mummy'. A day or so later Joyce appeared to Tricia again – patted her on the back and told her not to worry about her health – the symptoms did not indicate serious heart problems. A few days later Tricia was given the results of a recent medical test, Joyce was right – the symptoms were 'Raynaud's' disease – easily treatable and not life threatening

There is an unbroken magnetic-type link between healer and patient which is never broken.

The case of Clare Caplan and Crohne's disease

Shortly after becoming 'healers' first Robert (our son) and then Joyce and I treated various horses that were owned by Morreen Caplan and her daughters Clare and Kay. These healings were fairly frequent and we saw the family quite often. Then it was announced that Clare was to marry Ian Blaskey, and early preparations began to be talked about. At this stage there was a great upset due to some serious illness that had begun to affect Clare. A family friend, who was a surgeon, carried out several tests and advised cancellation of the wedding and an immediate operation for cancer etc.

Understandably her parents were distraught and asked us if we could help. We suggested that Clare should come and stay with us for a week or so during which time we would give her lots of healing. This was agreed and she duly stayed with us for a week or two. During this time the surgeon or his wife importuned Clare's parents saying it was vital that Clare should have the operation or the consequences could prove fatal. At the end of this period of constant healing sessions we told Clare's parents that we thought she was now better and suggested they should perhaps consult a non-surgical specialist away from Sheffield and any connection with their previous specialist. They did and the London specialist said it was not cancer, but Crohne's disease and that it was now cured.

The wedding went ahead and healthy children have been born and are now young adults. Clare and her family are well and very healthy

I do not think that they see very much of that particular surgeon! Clare's parents told us later that they decided to trust us with their daughter because we had been successful with their horses even sometimes after their vets had recommended that certain horses should be destroyed as being beyond help.

The case of Mrs Davy

This lady came unannounced with a friend, Heather Munn, who was having healing for multiple sclerosis. She was elderly and was suffering from several complaints; osteo-arthritis, heart, angina (had had a coronary attack previously), hyper-tension, and in addition had her right foot in a carpet slipper because it was so swollen. Her stomach was also very swollen and when she was sitting it came almost to her knees.

Heather asked us to heal her old friend before we started on her, and this we did. After treating all her complaints, I suggested that she should take various steps to improve her basic health; and suggested that she should come again in two weeks, by which time; hopefully she would have lost some excess weight.

She had come on a Monday; on the following Thursday both Joyce and I had felt very drained and tired generally so that we even resorted to having spoonfuls of honey. When she came again she looked to be a very different woman. Her right foot was in a normal shoe; she was full of energy, slimmer and obviously better. I therefore said 'my word, but you look a lot different and better'. To which she replied, 'Well you were there when they did the operation'. When I asked her to explain she told us that on the night of Wednesday, (when we had felt so tired on the Thursday) following her treatment by us on the Monday, she had gone to bed as usual. She was wakened from sleep by a group of white coated doctors, who removed her spirit from her body, then opened up her chest, took out her heart and cleaned it up before returning it to her chest cavity. She had then gone back to sleep but had experienced all the normal post operative feelings on the following days. She was now restored in energy; her foot was OK, and she had not had any angina symptoms and thank you both very much indeed.

Heather told us that she lived many years after this miracle spirit operation.

The case of the three sleepy people from Leeds 17.03.83

The party of three came by appointment; they were a Mrs Audrey Whincup, and Mr & Mrs Roy and Gisella Dennis. Although they had made an appointment, they arrived early, due no doubt to the difficulty of estimating how long it would take to come from Leeds. I therefore asked Joyce to take into the dining room the patients we were just finishing, and after they had gone would she be kind enough to bring in some tea for these three people from Leeds. When Joyce came in with a tray of tea some 15 to 20 minutes later she found all three of them fast asleep, having 'dropped off' to sleep during my healing.

Mrs Whincup suffered from cancer of the bone marrow following breast cancer and we had been treating her by absent healing since 28th of December 1982, she lived until 9th December 1984.

The complaint of Roy Dennis was heart problems, while Gisella (who was German) was tense through worry about her husband.

A fortnight after we treated Roy, we heard that Roy had felt first a cold needle in his heart and then a very hot needle in his heart and later when examined by his doctor, he found his heart to be alright. They attended for further healing from time to time in the following year and they would all fall asleep within 5 or 10 minutes of sitting down in our lounge – hence the title.

We still get Christmas cards from the Dennis's.

The case of Angela Dethick (daughter of Joe and Edith Hill) 24.11.88

Angela had married James Dethick who turned out to be the son of Nelson whom he had not seen since his separation from his wife shortly after his son's birth. Quite a coincidence!

She came on Joe's recommendation for infertility. Although they had had a child some three years previously, they had been unable to have a second child although the doctors could not find any reason. She had treatment from me on the 24th of November 1988. Joe reported in mid January 1989 that Angela had become pregnant but that she had been frightened by a savage Alsatian guard dog and had miscarried.

So she had further healing on 16th January 1989 and six or seven weeks later was declared to be pregnant again with morning sickness etc. for which she had spiritual healing. On the 25th of October 1989 Joe told me that Angela had had her new baby and all was well.

On the 4th November 1992 it was trouble again; Angela had fibroids. So of course she came for spiritual healing for that but told me she had made an appointment to see a consultant on the 27th November. After the healing she felt very much better and said that she would phone me after seeing the specialist. The specialist could not find any fibroids and she is now very well.

The case Mrs Barbara Fitzherbert

In the early 1960's when I was the manager of the main branch of the bank in Derby, I had a telephone message from the bank's Deputy Chairman, a Mr Cuthbert Fitzherbert. He wanted me to appoint a photographer to take a series of photographs of a special property in Norbury, near Ashbourne in Derbyshire. It was apparently the previous home of a member of the Fitzherbert family and it had become vacant through the death of the last incumbent. By the rules governing the Trust that controlled it, he could have been the next occupant – but he could not afford to take it on and carry out all the repairs and modernisation that it would require. So it was going to be the privilege of a relation who was farming somewhere farther south. What he was wanting for the family records were photographs of 'before and after'. I told him that I was an able camera user and offered to do the necessary work and this I did to very good effect and he was very appreciative. The effect was that we became quite close friends not withstanding the difference in our social and bank positions. Towards the end of the exercise he told me that his dear wife had been diagnosed as having breast cancer and that it was being treated through specialists in Reading.

After I had transferred to the Sheffield main branch and came to live in Hathersage he told me that he often came to the same area to take care of the special Chapel near Grindleford, the Padley Chapel for which he was a trustee. It had great historical interest and involved the martyrdom of two Jesuit priests. There are beautiful wall decorations dating from those troubled times. He called on one of these visits and told me with great sorrow that his wife's cancer had reappeared as secondaries in the bone marrow of her thigh bone and hip. I told him of our healing ability and offered to give treatment if they could accept it. I said this because he was a very dedicated high-ranking Roman Catholic and I thought it might clash with his beliefs. But no, he was very glad to accept and we, Joyce and I, went to where they had come to live in a village near Ashbourne, it was called Norbury.

It was a large detached house with a large garden of which Barbara was very proud and in which she did a lot of gardening. We then gave her healing, after we had enjoyed a very nice luncheon and a lot of pleasant conversation, Cuthbert left the room and came back with the various medicines that Barbara had to take. After she had finished the lot, Cuthbert said 'It is now time for your siesta. Off you go for your lie down'. To which Barbara replied 'I'm not going to bed, I'm going into the garden. After my healing I feel full of energy, so I'm going out into the garden to do some work that needs doing'.

Shortly after this healing Cuthbert took his wife back to see their specialist so that he could monitor her condition. Cuthbert said the specialist was astonished by her improvement and said the cavity in her bone marrow had been made good, and he could not account for it. So Cuthbert told him of the healing and said they had also prayed. The specialist said that must have been the cause; nothing he had been able to do would have been able to restore the bone marrow cavity. They were understandably overjoyed. Barbara was a very lovely lady and she was given every possible support by her loving husband. We exchanged Christmas cards for many years after that and we cherished their friendship.

The case of Storry Greaves and his daughter Helen's pony 'Tic Tack'.

Storry came for healing at the suggestion of his nephew, Michael in October 1996. He had lived on his father's farm at Worrall and had contracted rheumatic fever when he was about 18 years old. As I began attuning to Storry, I had a very strong impression of Harry Edwards. He told me of his early illness and how Harry Edwards had been treating him; first by absent healing then contact. His mother had asked Harry Edwards for absent healing without telling him, and he had wondered why he could see spirit figures around his bed when he was seriously ill. Because he took a long time feeling only half alive he made an appointment to go and see Harry Edwards at his healing sanctuary at Shere near Guilford. He drove himself there and it took him four rests to get there. After Harry had healed him he drove all round Rickmansworth and then all the way home in one unbroken journey without any problems.

Early in 1999 he rang to ask me to give absent healing to his daughter Helen's pony 'Tic Tack', which was stabled in a farm near where she worked in Scotland in Ballater. The pony was 27 years old and was finding difficulty in getting up after rolling etc. It got so that the vet was called. With a struggle he was placed in a sling and the vet thought he might well have to put him 'down'. The following morning when he got there, however, (after the absent healing) he found the pony trotting round the farmyard and in much better condition than for a long time.

On the 4th March 1999, a Sunday morning, Michael Greaves rang me to ask for help. His Uncle Storry had rung him by mobile phone from the horse box in which he was bringing 'Tic Tack' back home to Worrall. At the time he rang they were on the A74 somewhere short of Carlisle. Storry reported that 'Tic Tack' was so unstable he did not think he would survive even as far as Carlisle. I duly did as requested and asked to be advised of the outcome. On Monday morning the 15th Storry rang me to report; it had been a journey of twelve hours, he had stayed in the box section the whole way singing and talking to 'Tic Tack'. Apparently, after the absent healing he had calmed down completely, gained balance and strength, and had munched hay etc. A complete change! He was now none the worse for his ordeal and was to be seen trotting around the farm in high spirits. Storry even sang me two of the old songs that he had sung to the pony.

I think Storry had missed his true vocation!!

The story of Mike Hammond

Contact with Mike came through Peter Schofield who worked for our John in his market garden enterprise. He was

165

a part-time or week-end Park Ranger, and Mike Hammond was Head Ranger. Peter had benefited from my healing after spraining his wrist and thumb while climbing on the Stannage rocks and he had told Mike of the healing.

Mike came to me in March 1981 with an old back injury or sacroiliac ache. He responded very well and later brought his 13 year old Alsatian bitch for treatment. Its back legs were beginning to collapse. The dog was better immediately and worked in rescues for a further two years. In 1991 or thereabouts Mike had brought his wife and some other friends for various healings, all with very good results. Then in 1994 he was going to take and lead an expedition to Spitzbergen. He asked what he could do if ever he was in trouble with his back or indeed any other form of danger. I told him that he could make contact with me mentally and he would receive help as though I were actually with him.

While he was away I kept him on my absent healing list and one day, when I felt a surge of healing going away from me without knowing to whom it was going I made a note in my diary. When Mike returned from this expedition he contacted me to say 'thank you for your help during my expedition'. Apparently he had taken his party in a small boat to cross a very cold sea inlet. The boat had become stuck on an obstruction and nothing succeeded in freeing them. So he knew that he had to get into the water and physically push it off whatever was holding them. He also knew that he could not survive in that cold water for longer than, say eight or nine minutes. He remembered what I had told him and called on me for help, and then he roped up and jumped into the icy water, pushed the boat free and was hauled back to safety.

When he sat down in the boat - I was sitting next to him, giving him healing. When they got to the shore he re-heated himself with the Chinaman's circle!

After several more expeditions, including one to Alaska, he took another group of potential leaders to Spitzbergen. Here he was again in trouble. They were crossing a glacier of considerable area, when a mist came down which obliterated all visibility. His compass did not seem to work properly and eventually he had to admit that he was lost. His party said 'Come on Mike, what are you going to do now to get us to safety?' He promptly did his mental contacting with me and asked for help and directions. He got a very clear message from me, which told him to take a specified direction and walk for 22 minutes; after which would be clear sunshine. With every confidence, he gave this instruction to his party and they were in sunshine and safe within twenty minutes, he was most grateful.

On each occasion they had occurred at the times I had experienced the sudden flow of healing.

The case of Joe Hill, his wife Edith and Fleur his prize Fresian

This connection was introduced by a friend, on 2nd February 1988, Fay Plant and continues to this day. He came first with a seriously painful right knee which was aggravated by his work as a stone-waller. He had had a bad stroke in 1987 and was taking various drugs, such as Warfarin. He had an irregular pulse, a hiatus hernia and poor circulation to the left hand.

He responded well, as did Edith, who had complained of pain in the left upper arm and shoulder; a strange birth mark on the left hand also became better and not painful.

Joe, over the succeeding years had spells of trouble including cystitis, bladder weakness, eyes etc and in 1990 was treated for his hiatus hernia which responded immediately and has not troubled him since.

In March Edith was involved in an accident ending with bruises and she felt better after healing.

During the early part of 1988 Joe came with a request that we should heal his prize winning Fresian cow 'Fleur' which was starting to have aborting trouble, losing her calves before birth. She was treated in a barn after the rest of the herd had been brought in for milking. After a short time of actual on hands healing over the pelvis area, she suddenly let her milk release and my feet were soaked with her milk. Fleur was better, however, and went on to have some more prize-winning calves.

There were frequent minor healings due to the fact that he brought his friend Nelson Dethick on a weekly basis for his healing for sight problems and diabetes(see separate account of his experience with us) On the 12th March 2000, a Sunday, his wife Edith rang to ask for help for Joe. He had developed a stone in the kidney and was in great pain which pain killers did not help. I gave him absent healing and shortly after he was free from pain. When he attended on the following Wednesday with Nelson Dethick I gave him hands-on healing. While I was doing this Nelson was in trance after his healing. He always saw his parents and grandparents while in this state and when he resurfaced he told us that Joyce had been with them and he had introduced her to his family. She had also said that the healing I had given Joe would prove successful.

The following day Joe had a heavy discoloured discharge when emptying his bladder and the following day he had further scans with x-ray and ultrasound. To everybody's delight he was absolutely clear and there had not been any further pain or other symptoms.

The story of Joe Hill and his family including Nelson Dethick connected through the marriage of their children

In 1988 they brought their grandson Edward James for therapy. He suffered from asthma and had a hole in the heart. I think he was aged about 7 or 8 years. After treatment he was absolutely O.K. and he reported to Joe that Mr B. was a good bloke!
He next came in February 1992 with badly aching knees. He was O.K. after healing.

In June 1990, Joe's youngest son, Christopher John, was taken seriously ill with an infection in his left arm. Although on anti-biotics he got worse and it was diagnosed as septicaemia and Joe rang me from the hospital saying that nothing seemed to be helping his son, and he thought he might die. We gave absent healing immediately and the crisis passed and he recovered. His wife Fran came for healing later that year and also was better from problems involving kidneys and liver following a hysterectomy.

George Nelson Dethick   (his son married Angela Hill)

Joe brought Nelson Dethick for treatment in July 1990. He
was suffering from diabetes, which had affected his eyes and
circulation to his feet. Bleeding behind the eyes had caused
blindness and he had lost his driving licence. He sat on the
treatment stool and within a short time he suddenly
exclaimed that he could see the birds in the back garden. On
his way home his sight further improved so that he could
easily see the sign posts etc. Two months later he got his
driving licence back! He was under the care of an eye
surgeon Mr Mohammed at Calow hospital. Chesterfield.
When he saw him on a routine appointment, he told him what
had occurred and to his surprise this seemed to anger Mr
Mohammed, who said he was not finished with his treatments
because he had a cataract on his left eye which would require
surgery. This took place in October 1990 and a student was
allowed to do the surgery; there was a massive haemorrhage
and he was blinded in the left eye!

He also had healing to sores on his toes and feet that seemed
difficult to treat effectively by the Bakewell Hospital. All
these troubles subsided without any further escalation. His
feet are now in very good condition.

There is more to tell of this particular patient. When
treatment starts he very soon slips into a trance state. This
will last for 30 – 55 minutes. During this time Joyce, who is
a clairvoyant, would see that he was being seen by his parents

and grandparents and sometimes other people who were still on the Earth Plane and not, as others, in Spirit.

After Joyce had passed over some two weeks, she joined Nelson and his relations. He 'woke up' to tell us that they had had a lovely time together and she had told him that the healing to Joe's kidney would prove successful (I had been giving Joe the healing while Nelson was 'away' and so it turned out. On the next day he had a great deal of discoloration in his urine and the doctor's x-ray showed his kidney was clear.

The case of Graham Horridge – friend of Joe Hill

He came to us on the recommendation of his old pal Joe Hill. They had both been stone walling together (Joe being so good that he was a judge for competition stone- walling)

He came early in February 2000 with concern for the loss of sight that he was experiencing. He was only 53 – 54 years old, had had 20/20 vision and was upset to think he was losing it, particularly as it was affecting his ability to paint his pictures.

I gave him treatment to his eyes, neck area, shoulders etc. and told him of the exercise he should do to keep his eyes healthy, and he went on his way home to Cheshire. He telephoned me a week later to tell me he had experienced a miracle on his way home. Apparently he had passed through Glossop and when he approached Staley Bridge his eyes had suddenly filled with tears. He had to stop and mop up all the moisture to be able to see, and to his surprise and delight he could see brilliantly.

When he got home it was quite dark and when he entered his well lit home he was amazed at how brilliant everything appeared. He did not say anything to his wife however in case it was just a flash-in-the-pan, as they say, but it was still the same in the following days – so he told her then and then he rang to tell me. He subsequently sent me a letter telling me all was still 'brilliant' and he was very grateful for the healing he had received.

The case of David Keeton

David came to us first, one day after his 15th birthday (16.11.81). He was a student at Repton Public school and was suffering from a malignant tumour of the brain. It was inoperable and he had been on a course of chemotherapy – which had caused hair loss etc. After treatment he very quickly showed improvement. He was seen by the Children's Hospital, Sheffield who decided that he would be strong enough to withstand further chemotherapy treatment and this was started. He was also a private patient of Anthony Jefferson neurologist.

On the start of fresh chemotherapy, David started to show signs of rapid deterioration. At his next visit to Anthony Jefferson (famous brain surgeon) he asked what they were doing to have caused this. When they told him what the Children's Hospital were doing, Jefferson asked for their appointment card and tore it up, telling them not to have any more chemotherapy.

He rapidly came back to improving again and was soon back at school. He now runs a Public House with restaurant and is very healthy. It is now some 21 years since he was told the bad news about his malignant growth.

The case of Gerald Mackie 23.12.86

One day, as it was approaching Christmas, a friend who had benefited from our healing asked if she could bring a friend of hers who lived in Switzerland. We said yes, of course and this man duly arrived along with his teenage children with Clare as guide and chauffeuse.

He had been suffering for seven years from severe headaches, the cause of which had not been diagnosed even though he had spent many visits to the Mayo Clinic in New York (flying there for the purpose). We suggested that his family should go off for a long walk and then proceeded to give healing. He responded well and said he felt great heat on his head and his eyes. There appeared to be great 'excitement' in my spirit guides. We then put him on our large settee where he promptly fell asleep. He slept for 45 minutes or so. When he eventually woke up he said he felt wonderfully different and very much encouraged. He asked if he could have absent healing while still at home and we said that we would be pleased to synchronise the time and collaborate.

He then said his heartfelt thanks and asked how much he owed us for his healing. I told him that I did not charge, but that he could make a donation if he wished and that this would be used to give to my charities. At this he took out a roll of paper money, stripped three notes off the roll and stuffed them into my breast pocket. When he had gone I found out that they were each for £50.00, a big lift for my charities!

We continued absent healing for some time and he rang to tell us that he felt the same sensations, including sleep, as he had felt when he had contact healing. He said he was very much better. Finally we gave him a telephone number of the Referral Service of the National Federation of Spiritual Healers who gave him the names of four Healers based in Bern, Switzerland, and places near his home. We also arranged to continue the absent healing at 'bedtime'. He rang again in two weeks time to say he was now very well.

The case of Mary Matthews and her mystery cold shoulder

Early in our ministry of healing we were approached by Mr and Mrs Matthews. She was suffering from an original problem of cold shoulder. In the course of several months the doctor had tried various treatments without success and she had been referred to the neurological specialist Mr Gumpert (the same Mr Gumpert who was involved with our other patient Maurice Womersley).

The recommendation was to have all her teeth extracted. After this it came about that Mary could not manage with the false teeth with which she was fitted. After three sets of different teeth, she came to us. We gave her the usual treatments and she seemed to make some progress. However she was still taking the drugs that were prescribed by Mr Gumpert. When her other symptoms did not improve he gave her increased dosages.

Eventually the quantity was sufficient that a whole packet, including the guidance notes were supplied to Mr Matthews. He read the notes and found that the drug should not be given for longer than a very limited period. The awful fact was that they had already exceeded the maximum period. The instructions said that if the period was exceeded then the following circumstances would be inevitable. I cannot remember the actual prophesied effects but she was already experiencing them, (blackouts was one I believe).

When Mr Matthews took the paper to Mr Gumpert, all he said was well you might as well continue now, it can't be undone.

She went into hospital shortly afterwards where she died. The family were absolutely devastated. But no action was taken against the specialist.

The case of the Indian boy (five years of age) called Aseef Merali

This case was referred to me through an introduction via the NFSH (National Federation of Spiritual Healers), to whom the parents had applied for help. They were in business in Sheffield and their son, Aseef, was going blind with an eye complaint which was untreatable. It was certain that he would be blind by nine years of age – eleven at the maximum. There was a belief and knowledge of Spiritual

Healing in both parents and they had read of the NFSH.

The eyesight was already deteriorating and to see the T.V he had to sit only one foot away, and that with very thick lenses in his spectacles. We therefore gave healing, mostly to the head and eyes, and he seemed to Joyce to have made a change in the colour of his aura. Noted at the time was the fact that husband and wife were of different castes. The father was of high caste and his wife was low caste. She had different very beautiful shaped scull and face. They had had to elope to get married and had defied their racial customs in doing so.

After a pleasant stay they took their leave only to come back after a few minutes to say they had not paid. We explained that we did not charge for our help and they were suitably grateful.

When they came on their next visit it was to report that there had been an improvement in Aseef's eyesight and they brought a gift as a thank you. It was a carved part elephant tusk. It had been brought by them when the family escaped from Idi Amin in East Africa. The part tusk had been carved very nicely to show an African face and is now one of our treasured possessions.

After four visits Aseef's eyesight became normal and he could see perfectly well without glasses. As a result we had visits from their family relations some of whom had come especially from the East, Kenya and parts of India. The grandfather came and tested Aseef by sending him to the far end of our lounge (31feet) and asked him to say how many fingers he was holding up. He was right every time.

I remember one of the female members of the family came for healing for her knees, and she lifted up her skirts to reveal her long under-garments that are like loose trousers tied at the ankle.

In 1998 I tried to find out how Aseef was and traced an uncle – still in Sheffield. He told me that Aseef was now back in Africa, in Tanganyika and with perfect eyesight.

The case of Sheena Miller and husband Mike

The Millers came to me in September 1978, but I cannot now remember how they had heard about our healing.

She was suffering from very high blood pressure and with kidney failure. Her doctors had felt that the condition was perhaps the result of the side effects of having taken the contraceptive pill for some years. They had told her that she had only a maximum of five years to live. She had had problems with her first husband and had remarried fairly recently. She was on medication for her kidneys and for blood-pressure.

She responded well to healing and after several visits she had seen her doctor who had found her blood pressure had changed completely and it was now low. They had had to take her off the medication for that part of her treatment and they also found that her kidneys were now back to normal - which they could not understand. In the past the doctors had warned her not to get pregnant because it would have put further pressure on her kidneys. Now that she was so much better she and her husband felt it would be very nice if they could start a family. They tried but were unable to achieve the desired result – so came for fertility treatment.

They reported in November 1979 that they were expecting a baby and were delighted with their success after all the warnings they had had. A baby girl was safely delivered on 14th April 1980 and they called her Sophie Louise. When she was about six months old Sheena and Mike brought her to us so that we could share in their joy and happiness. As they came into our lounge carrying Sophie, the little girl held out her arms to Joyce and me as though she already knew us. It was an emotional moment.

After many years of exchanging Christmas cards and lovely photographs, on the 29th October 1999 we had a letter from Sophie reminding us of the past and telling us that she was about to start a course at Durham University. Because of the circumstances of her mother's illness and her birth she was very interested in the Spiritual side of life and was to take 'the paranormal' as one of her subjects. Her photographs show her as a very lovely girl/young woman and her personality matched her looks.

We look forward to seeing her and her parents in the future.

The case of Thomas and Diana Montgomery

They first came in 1977 and Thomas was the patient. He had had a T.B. lung section surgically removed. This had left him with neck, shoulder and left arm pains, and mobility problems. He responded very well and was completely OK.

A few weeks later Diana came with some back trouble and this was also treated with complete success.

Some three years later she came back with a return of the back aches. On her second visit, after treatment, we sat and talked and I told her that I had had a spirit message to the effect that my healing would be speeded up and become more effective. At this she said 'Then I wish you would do something about my left elbow'. This had never been mentioned in any of our previous meetings. Apparently she had dislocated her left elbow some 14 years previously while playing with her little daughter. At that time she had been treated by a doctor at the Manchester hospital, who had left the elbow in a neck sling for some weeks. Eventually when the sling was removed it was found that the elbow was locked and would not extend beyond the right-angle position.

After complaining and begging them not to leave her in that restricted condition they eventually got the elbow joint to relax by a few degrees; it had been like that for 14 years.

I told her that I felt I could help her and began to feel 'energised' so that I was tingling all over. I held my hands around, but not touching, her elbow, and her fingers began to move about. Then I made contact with the joint and slowly stroked both hands down her arm and off her fingers. Whereupon the arm went straight, she exclaimed with delight 'Look Tommy – same length' as she extended both arms in front of her. That was some twenty years ago and she had not had any trouble since.

There was a lovely incident about two years later when my wife and I were in the Chatsworth Garden Centre looking at cane furniture. There was a sudden squeal of delight and Diana was bearing down on me with her arms outstretched saying 'Look – still the same length'. She gave me a welcoming hug; fortunately both our better halves were present!

The case of Jan Murphy (in Canada)

In the early days of 1973 Joyce and I went on holiday to Scotland with the man who was to succeed me as manager of my branch bank, and his wife. He asked us to call and see his Aunt who had a son who also had been diagnosed as having muscular dystrophy. This was at the early age of eight or nine and he had been taken to see all kinds of specialists. They had all said let him do whatever pleases him; he will not have long to live so do whatever makes him feel happy.

They had finally taken him to a recluse-like man in an out of the way village in Devon; all the way by taxi from Annan in Scotland. This 'healer' had held him in his arms and asked if they were hoping for a miracle. They had answered 'Yes' and they had come all the way home again by the taxi. After that the father had massaged him every day with sea weed water and they had had a church prayer group praying for him specially – and here he now was at the age of twenty-one and quite normal.

When his Aunty Bunny Brookfield heard of our gift of healing she asked if we would do absent healing for her niece, Jan Murphy, who lived in Canada. She had had many operations for cancer; had three children and was only in her early 30's; and had been told that she had only a few months to live.

We duly carried out the absent healing.

Some years later after I had retired and Frank was the manager of my old branch, I called to cash a cheque and saw Bunny Brookfield, who had been visiting her nephew. I asked her how Jan was and how the healing had affected her. To my delight she said that her niece had lived another twelve years and had visited her in Scotland several times before she had died.

Letter of Acknowledgement

Annan
Dumfriesshire
14.09.74

Dear Alan
Thank you for your letter with news of you all and of John. Jan is really keeping quite well, she has been home for three weeks and I took her to our healing service on Wednesday morning. She is certainly looking so much better but unfortunately her last operation (which was to put the bowel back) cannot be done, but she is a remarkable girl and a real fighter, surely after nearly four years, she must have to be healed of the cancer, her surgeon in Canada has never known anyone who has lasted so long and we all feel sure it is through the prayers of so many. Jenny (her mother) is also more relaxed and we should like to say thank you to you and all your friends for the time you take in prayer.
We had a wonderful three weeks in Canada with my son, daughter-in-law and grandchildren. What a joy it was to see

Michael swimming with them and yet only 20 years ago we were told he only had a little while to live – he has got his PHD now and is a Professor at Guelpa University with a lovely family and home. My daughter is expecting her first baby in January so we are all very thrilled about it. We miss seeing Robert and Caroline growing up but we cannot have everything. We are lucky we see them every year and a few phone calls as well.

We always remember John in our prayers – our list is always long but what amazing results we see and hear of. What a wonderful gift you and Joyce have got even more wonderful that you use it to help. Rene wrote and said she was going to stay with John did she tell you about their cousin Brenda, who had made a disastrous marriage? Perhaps you would remember her in your prayers.

Frank sends his best wishes to you both.

Love to Joyce and family. Will let you know more details of Jan when I have her next letter. She is back in Hamilton, Ontario now and family near my family, who are going to see. Thank you again.

Bunny Brookfield

The case of Mrs Ruby Muxlow

This started as a result of my giving a talk on Spiritual Healing to the members of the United Reform Church in Totley Brook Road, Totley Rise, Sheffield in 1983. Incidentally I had arranged to give the talk one year earlier – but my mother-in-law died suddenly on the actual day and I had to cancel.

In my talk I had mentioned the healing skills of the great Harry Edwards who had demonstrated at the Sheffield City Hall. I quoted the case of his treatment for a Derbyshire Neck which had responded immediately so that the great lump in her throat had dispersed – and everyone had seen it happen.

At the interval for coffee and biscuits Ruby Muxlow approached from her position on the front row of the audience where she had been sitting still wearing her outdoor clothes (it was October, and cold). She smiled and said 'Do you know what I want?' I said I thought she wanted my card so that she could come and see me and this I gave with my right hand. She took it with her right hand and I touched her 'comfortingly' on the right wrist with my left hand.

It was some five or six weeks before she actually came for healing (brought by her daughter who was a theatre sister in hospital)(and would not stay in the house with her mother). She asked me if I remembered what I had done to her and I was able to tell her precisely. Her Derbyshire neck was the biggest I had ever seen. It involved her throat and upper chest, and was in-operable, because it had spread into vital parts of throat, vocal chords, etc. She told me that she had delayed her visit until she had been able to see her specialist, a Professor Munro of the Northern General Hospital. He had seen her with a circle of student doctors to whom he had explained that she was an especially interesting case. She had had a thrombosis in the right arm some 14 years previously which had resulted in her losing the pulse from her right wrist. She had been a 'blue baby'; had heart problems; was always cold and could not walk more than 100 yards on the flat. As the Professor was saying this he began feeling her left wrist pulse, then passed to her other wrist explaining to his students that she had no pulse here and suddenly said 'Good God, there's a pulse again'.

She then told me that not only had that happened but that the ulcer (varicose) on her leg had gone, leaving no scar; the bunion on the left foot had gone; and she was able to walk up Totley Rise, do her shopping and walk home without getting out of breath. She continued to make further progress, was a delightful personality and dined out on the experience for a long time. It was also noticed that her string of pearls which previously had merely gone around her goitre now extended below her waist. She passed to spirit very peacefully some five years later at an advanced age.

The case of Deborah Oddy

This patient came to me on the recommendation of two of my existing patients. She was 18 weeks into a new pregnancy and had been troubled by pains in the area of her gall bladder. The doctors had found that she had gall stones which in the ordinary way would have been removed by keyhole surgery, except for the danger of harming the unborn child. But she was having some frequent pain at a fairly serious level. Painkillers were not recommended in case they affected the pregnancy. She had also developed Gestational diabetes – this additional complication was something from which she had suffered on earlier pregnancies.

I started by giving Absent Healing until she could attend in person. She finally came on the 26th February 2001. She reported that the pain had ceased with the Absent Healing and it had not recurred. She responded well to contact healing and we concentrated on treating the gall bladder. She had cancelled an appointment of two months ahead as she was feeling much better; the pain had not returned and a second opinion had reported an improvement in the various problem areas; and the infection in the Gall Stone tube had much reduced. The doctors were loath to operate before the birth and were satisfied that it would be safe to await the birth, which was to be by 'caesarean section' in July.

A beautiful baby boy was safely delivered on the 11th July. They have named him Joshua Matthew. All went well and the gall stones were 'calm'. She finally attended with baby on 7th December 2001 and said the doctors had discovered a large cyst on the left ovary when doing the caesarean but that too was not operated on in all the circumstances. So we gave her healing for that and for the gallstones. Later that month she reported that they were not to operate on the cyst as it had shrunk so very considerably.

Finally she called again to say that all was well – the gall stones had disappeared; the ovary cyst was also of no further trouble and we were able to say that the Case was Closed.

The story of Ray Ollerenshaw and 'The Grapevine' free newspaper

Ray lived locally and had been a sheep farmer in the Hope Valley for most of his life, one of his farms had overlooked the Derwent Reservoir, but when I first treated him he had come to live in Hathersage. He was quite famous for his part in the long running TV series 'One man and his dog'. His second wife, Betty, was the President/Chairman of the Derwent Women's Institute and I had given her club talks on Spiritual Healing. When Ray became ill with angina and some other heart trouble she brought him to me for treatment and this was successful.

Because of his fame as a TV personality he was approached by the Editor of a free monthly newspaper called 'The Grapevine'. It was distributed all over North Derbyshire, Nottinghamshire and South Yorkshire; this included Sheffield South. It was delivered over a very wide area and was obviously paid for by the advertising it carried.

It was a very interesting and sensitively written article with photographs. Apparently Ray told him about me and my Spiritual Healing capabilities and so he approached me with the request that he be allowed to do a feature on me. I told him that I would be very happy to co-operate on such an enterprise provided that he investigated actual cases after I had obtained permission from each patient to publicise their cases. And also that he would report the facts absolutely straight and this he readily agreed to do.

I was able to obtain several patients who were happy to co-operate and they came to my home or he went to theirs until he had got enough for a full range of different types of case. All of this took several weeks and eventually he asked me to grant him permission to attend at my convenience so that he could get a professional photographer to take snaps of me to print on his front page. The photographer used up two whole spools before he finally said he was satisfied he had a suitable shot. This turned out to be one which had been taken with him lying on the floor while I stood on top of the piano stool. Joyce thought it was hilarious and brought lots of tea and cakes to keep us refreshed.

The paper came out at the end of November 1991 and had some immediate, almost shattering results. Our telephone was never silent; we had up to fifty patients a week; at the end of two weeks we had a telephone call from a hospital patient in Toronto (he had received the newspaper from relatives who lived in Sheffield) who had cancer and only two weeks to live. With absent healing he lived three months and we had a busy exchange of letters.

Slowly the impact began to wear off but in that year I believe we saw 2,500 patients (some of which were repeats of course). Because I made no charge, most wanted to make a voluntary donation which I saved and passed on to many charities. It amounted to £1,000 to £1,500 per annum and I have kept careful records to be able to prove, if necessary, that I did not benefit myself (for tax purposes).

On one occasion six elderly ladies who had been treated for bad knees, backs etc. asked about paying and finally insisted on giving a contribution; they each left a 10 pence piece in my collection box. I thought that was very touching and reminded me of 'the widows mite'.

There were some quite funny reports from patients about the way they would use the photograph from the paper. One old lady who had chest problems always went to bed with it pinned to her nightie. Apparently it was very comforting and effective.

Sadly Ray passed away resting in his Land Rover after winning a dog trial on 10th July 1993.

The case of Mandy Jane Palmer

This patient was the second of its type – that of an 'S' shaped curvature of the spine. She was about eleven to twelve years old and the right side of the body was affected. Not only was there an 'S' curvature but also a twist along the upper spine so that the rib cage was concave in the lower ribs on the right side. This was exactly the same as the girl from Leeds who was the daughter of an architect colleague of our friend Bill Gower. This girl was operated on the day before a demonstration by Harry Edwards in the City Hall, Sheffield. This we attended and she was asked for by Harry Edwards who had been approached by her parents as a possible case for his demonstration.

In this later case we had treated Mandy for about six or eight weeks with noticeable improvements and had advised her parents to contact Harry Edwards as in the previous case. This time they accepted an invitation to attend a public demonstration in Stafford Town Hall and we were invited to go along to see what happened.

The Town Hall was packed, balcony and all available seats. Joyce could see that the stage was occupied by about sixty 'blue' spirit figures. In addition to Harry, there was Ray

Branch, his assistant, an osteopath and a doctor. There were many wonderful healings carried out in front of all eyes until the very last patient. Harry asked, 'is there anyone suffering from a curvature of the spine?' Young Mandy put up her hand and was called to the stage.

Harry sat her on a stool with her back to the audience and asked the osteopath to trace the course of the spine through her coat so that the audience could appreciate the extent of the problem. Then after a short pause Harry stood at her left side, Ray at her right side and simultaneously starting at shoulder level, persuaded the spine into a straight line. It was all over in a matter of minutes and Mandy came back to where we were in tears and emotionally deeply affected.

About a week later Mandy was brought back to us by her mother so that we could see the effect of the healing. In the previous healing sessions I had finished off the treatment by massaging the spine and whole of the back (as I had been taught to do for my son, John) and we were shown the spine. It was perfectly straight and the rib cage was also normal, having lost the concavity that had been there before. She used to wave to us on the odd occasion from the saddle of the pony she was riding. She married and has children, a great success for Spiritual Healing and for the great healer Harry Edwards.

The case of Mrs Jane Parker

This patient came from the Derby area, brought by her husband who was employed by Rolls Royce in a management capacity. First visit was 7th December 1976. She suffered from osteo-arthritis in very severe form, all limbs and all over the body. She came in carrying a big 'bean cushion' to sit on as she could not bear the pain of a normal chair. She came at 3.30 p.m. and the healing went on and on; interspersed by trays of tea from Joyce, until they left at 7 o'clock. There was a remarkable reaction and a steady improvement in pain level as the healing progressed. Finally all pain gone and feeling relaxed and overjoyed she went back home to take up house keeping again after having had to stay with her mother because she had been unable to cope with normal house work.

As she went out of the front door she said to her husband 'That was the most amazing ten minutes I have ever experienced'.

Some further treatments followed over the next two years but there was to be a very sad end. Her husband was sent out to Cairo by Rolls Royce for a period of work. She found out that he had taken up with a local beauty and did not want her to join him. After a few unsuccessful attempts at suicide she finally threw herself under a train near her home in Sponden and was killed instantly.

During her contacts with us she wrote the following poem which I print in memory of a very lovely young woman:-

To Alan and Joyce by Jane Parker

Through distress to you I was brought
Where healing powers I sought
Together united, we were as one
Healing hands on me, The Sun Shone

Distraught, my legs so full of pain
My world unreal, happiness I did not feign.
I was received by Alan and Joyce,
His healing hands, her soothing voice.

A vision by Joyce is also seen,
Spirits to help; are described to me.
Through the medium, I'm allowed to escape
Helped by guides, it's not too late

Inadequate my words, of sensations that last,
Alan's healing power to me is passed.
No more to travel through despair.
Helped by you both, in your gifted care.

Jane Parker 1977

In appreciation of her healing Jane writes a long letter outlining her experience. It is as follows:-

My Experience by Jane Parker

During the middle of the summer of 1976 I was almost unable to walk with inflammation of the legs caused by rheumatism, which I had inadvertently caused by over taxing them. A doctor diagnosed my condition and reported that I would walk within two weeks. It is now May 1977 and I still have restrictions. However, in the autumn of 1976 I visited a medium; this was Alan and Joyce Bellinger, who were to play an important role in my recovery. My feelings at the time were almost complete disinterest, as I was too concerned with the pain I was coping with at the time. I must stress I did cling to hope.

191

We arrived; I had extreme pain and sat with great discomfort. Suddenly things started to happen. I had the most unusual feelings, a tingling with extreme hot and cold wherever Alan ran his hands over me. His wife also helped me by describing to me my faithful doctor who had passed away some ten years ago. I was not surprised to find Doctor Smith helping me as he had devoted a considerable amount of time to me, keeping me well in his lifetime.

I was asked to stand, supported by Alan and Joyce and felt this tremendous heat radiating from Alan. I became extremely hot. I must state that this heat stayed with me for at least two to three weeks. People commented on the heat radiating from me when they came in close contact with me. It was now winter and bitterly cold, but I did not feel the cold. I was very sorry when the heat treatment disappeared from me.

I also received treatment for my right leg, the weaker of the two. The right leg became very cold and this stayed with me for about a month. It would disappear and return at random. This also was a great comfort to me, for I had the feeling of being helped. The treatment was over a period of over two and a half hours I am told. My awareness of time was that five minutes had passed. I also had this beautiful floating feeling.

I must add that my right hip was treated. This also would go suddenly ice-cold for no apparent reason. If I related my experiences to someone I was aware of something happening to me. Mostly it was the feeling of someone pushing me in the small of the back.

I would like to move on to Christmas Day, but would like to comment that since my illness in the summer and early autumn I was almost unable to sit down, so therefore I had my legs up in bed for most of the time. If I walked it was with great pain, making it impossible to bear my own weight. Four months had passed; I was in bed on Christmas Day watching the morning service singing away and thanking God for being allowed a chance. My thoughts wandered to Alan and Joyce thanking them for all they had done for me. Closing my eyes I was suddenly aware of being very cold, in fact ice cold. It seemed to creep over me. I was in bed warm and suddenly the bed clothes went cold, my hands were white. I can only draw the conclusion that it was something to do connecting me with Alan and Joyce. I was so overwhelmed by this I told my husband and other relations, to make sure I had not imagined it. The cold feeling stayed with me for about half to three quarters of an hour. I would like to say I was not afraid, it was coming from Alan and Joyce and I wished them a Happy Christmas.

Time passed but progress was slow. I now have to relate a situation where my husband was called away abroad and I found myself in great distress. I could not stand sufficiently long enough to prepare myself a meal and therefore desolation set in. It was apparent I was not independent yet.

I went to bed and prayed with all my heart. I am sure I poured everything I'd got into my prayer. I prayed for strength to continue in these circumstances or for something positive to happen. The next morning I received a telephone call from my husband's office to say that the talks had broken down and he would be returning the same day. My husband was with me within 24 hours. Can we believe that prayer could be that powerful? I think the answer is YES.

I have visited Alan and Joyce twice more, once in late winter and once in early spring. All I can say is that every time I receive treatment, I am always aware of the tingling hot and cold feelings. Gradually the feelings are now fading but my legs are becoming stronger with every day. During this period of illness I also have found visiting my local swimming pool a great help. The water pressure seemed to do something. I must point out I only sat and perhaps did a few movements in the water

To draw a conclusion is almost impossible. Why? - is the inevitable question. But somehow I was directed to Alan and Joyce and was helped physically and mentally to regain most of my health and sincerely hope to recover completely.

The effort that was required to fight back to health was difficult but it was made considerably easier knowing that I was being helped by Alan and Joyce and for that I shall always thank them.

Affectionately yours
Jane

The case of Joe Scarborough (In the early 1970's)

I met this patient initially through the Caplans who knew him as a very up and coming artist of the Naïve School. He had done many things including being a miner, attendant at a Sheffield cinema etc.

His problem was irritable bowel syndrome. I asked him to sit on the treatment stool and proceeded to give healing from behind and rested my hands on his abdomen. After a short time the flow of healing stopped and he said that he had some strange feelings but would prefer to let me know how he felt after a few days.

I duly received a letter from Joe within a week. He had very distinctive writing and he said he need say no more than that he did not need the enclosed Hospital appointment card, as he was completely cured. He has not had any recurrence of the problem ever since and it is now 2001.

Letter of Acknowledgement

Langden Street
Sheffield
22.04.75

Dear Joyce and Alan
What a smashing day, thanks for everything. It was the sort of day Audrey and I shall savour for a long time; wasn't that Gaelic trifle something!
An added bonus was that I honestly haven't felt better in my life – no more bowel trouble – what a relief. It really has made me think. It's not really my habit to send rubbish into the countryside but I enclose my visiting card for the hospital and would be most pleased, if on our behalf, you could render it into many pieces.
The children slept like logs until school time and still carry rosy red cheeks.

Do look after yourselves as you have looked after us.
Joe and Audrey, Andrew and Rachel.

The case of Ken Strawson (1970/2)

This patient was a very interesting personality. He was a bank customer; a consultant on many engineering levels including hydraulics and electronics. His eldest son came to help my son, John, to erect the staging in his new, commercial size greenhouse. He was under the age of seventeen and therefore had to be delivered and collected by his father at the end of each days work. On one of these Ken came into the lounge dragging his left foot in some considerable pain. I asked him what was wrong and he told me that it was sciatica. I asked him what he had done about it. He replied **** What the h*** can you do bout it? He had been referred to hospital by his own doctor and they had tested him and tried everything over a period of three weeks without any success. They had finally told him to learn to live with it. I said perhaps I could help and asked him to sit on the treatment stool. This he did in some wonderment, after about 20 minutes he said all the pain had gone and he asked me what I had done; what was the science I had used; what was the equation for the energy? Etc.

So I tried to tell him about the way spiritual healing worked and how it had come to 'The Bellingers'. He asked many questions and I finally suggested that he should have a talk with my son Robert who was one year ahead of me. I also told him that Robert could have healing effects on delicate instruments just by holding them in his hands. So he agreed a time to come over again with his wife and with an instrument for testing electric current into which he would have created a fault – so that it could not work. At the subsequent meeting one evening, a few days later Joyce and I left Ken and Robert together while we went for a walk down the lane with his wife.

When we came back they were still talking and Ken was holding his meter instrument showing amazement that it would work now despite the fault he had put into it.

Some few days later I saw him at the bank and he told me that when he had got back to his works he had told his manager what had happened only to be told that his manager had also severed a contact within the instrument without telling Ken. So how could it work? They opened up the casing to find that the break had been re-soldered! He could not understand. But he sent me lots of new patients.

One was his secretary who had suffered a car accident in which she had hit her head on the windscreen (no seat belts at that time) and she had got whiplash and damage to the spinal cord. She could hardly walk and myelitis had been diagnosed. She came with her mother and in just a few minutes she was better, her colour came back and she was normal. Ken got a bottle of Gin as a thank you, we got only thanks!

He devised many instruments to control heavy cranes from tilting over, etc. and had a great sense of humour. He was 6' 5" tall and weighed 19+ stones. He was very strong and I saw him lift the rear end of a car clear off the ground.

He told me some funny stories about his father who was by

then a widower. He used to stay for periods of time with each of his several daughters and he would stir the feelings of each in turn against the others of the family.

Then he had a heart attack and was taken to Lodgemoor Hospital on the outskirts of Sheffield. The hospital rang Ken and said they were having trouble with his father. He was smoking. Ken said he had always smoked so what was wrong with that. They said 'but he's in an oxygen tent to save his life'.

Then they told him that he had assaulted a nurse who happened to be black. Apparently his father had woken up to find this black nurse at his bedside, he thought he had died and that he had gone to hell and that the nurse was either the devil himself or his deputy? So he kicked her in the face. The hospital told Ken that any more trouble and he would have to take his father out of their care.

The next event was even worse. His father had wanted to go to the toilet and did not like to use the bedpan. So he got out of bed and left the ward to find a toilet off the main central corridor. The hospital was designed with this very wide main corridor from which all the single storey wards went off, and they all looked alike. Then, when his father had used the toilet he wandered down the wrong ward, came to where his bed should have been only to find that there was another patient in it and he was wired up to all kinds of bottles and instruments. Without more ado, without asking any questions he threw this unfortunate man out of bed and got in himself. That was it!!

Ken used to ride a motorbike and when his father wanted to go on the pillion on a trip to the seaside Ken made him jump on while he was moving as otherwise the engine would stop!!!

Ken and his wife lived in a nice bungalow off the north side of Sheffield and he mentioned that he had had to rebuild his bed many times. He had finally resorted to using steel framing to withstand the combined weight of some 35 to 36 stones! They left our house one winter and he took a side road as a short cut just north of our home. It was very narrow and steep, and very icy. He was a very good, fast driver but by the time they had reached the main road his wife, Doreen, had pulled off the door handle from her door and the Mercedes he was driving was very strongly built!

He died from cancer which was all over his body and his last act was to give his wife a very knowing wink in reply to her farewell message of 'Love you'.

The story of Pauline Tickner

This lady came to us through an introduction from Joan Robson. Pauline was the wife of her husband's employer. She lived in Manchester (Didsbury) and was well to do. Her father had been a wealthy land owner in Norfolk, if I remember correctly, and her story of remarkable gifts started in the village where they lived. Apparently she was coming home from school one day and witnessed a motor car accident which involved a young woman who was injured. She immediately ran to the police station and gave the news to the sergeant in charge. He said, sit down and write a full detailed report of what you saw while it is still fresh in your memory. This she did, and then went home. Sometime later, that same day the sergeant called at their house and asked to see her father. He told her father that she had been wasting police time. She had reported an accident and when they got to the reported site there was nothing there, no accident. He was very cross and accused her of all sorts of nuisance, including that she was on drugs etc. Three weeks later the same sergeant called again and told them with amazement that the accident she had reported three weeks ago had just happened – every detail was as she 'had seen' it and had described in detail at the police station.

The date of her first visit was 7th June 1979 and she was suffering from stress and an aching back etc. Joyce knelt in front of her and held her hands while I treated her from behind. Joyce suddenly started to cry and tears were rolling down her cheeks. Pauline asked her what the matter was. Joyce replied that she could 'see' a perfect set of teeth and she felt ineffably sad for some unknown reason. Pauline then told us that it would be her mother – she had had a full set of perfect teeth when she died at the age of 89 years. And she was sure that it was her mother who was transmitting her sadness to Joyce. It was because Pauline had fallen-out with her very bright sister who was a barrister working in Switzerland. <u>This revelation caused Pauline to contact her sister and make friends again.</u>

Later she and a friend attended one or two of our Development Circles. She and her husband Colin went to India on a holiday trip and this included a visit to the Taj Mahal mosque. She wished that she could see the water and building without all the hoards of visitors that packed all sides of the water etc. After walking round the whole site once more, she declined to go round the interior and said she would just take a few snapshots of the mosque and then go back to the air-conditioned bus. The photographs she took came out <u>without any people showing</u> on the prints except for one silhouette (possibly herself); she gave me a copy for my records.

There were many more similar paranormal incidents with this patient; one such concerned her daughter, Anthea, who lived in Canada, in or near Toronto. It appeared that Anthea was very concerned about a friend whose surname was Heinz. This woman had been in Nazi concentration camp during the war and was now suffering from cancer. In fact, she had lost her hair and sight through the effects of the various radical treatments and was not expected to live for more than a few days.

Pauline had given us a photograph of this girl to help our absent healing. It showed a very attractive face and full head of curly hair. When Joyce 'saw' her in the 'O' she drew her without any hair and with blankets drawn up to her chin in bed. This amazed Pauline because this was how she was and how she slept. After absent healing she surprised Anthea by walking into her home, sight recovered and not in pain. She died peacefully about a month later.

During the Great War of 1939 – 1945 she had a very responsible job. She was head of the ATS, the women's army corps. After the war she married her Colin to look after him as he was not in very good health and needed her very good mind to help face the difficulties of life after the war.
While we were in contact over healing she told me of an interesting example of her special gifts. Apparently her husband was chairman of the local Conservatives where they

lived. Mrs Thatcher, the Prime Minister visited them on the AGM and spoke some heartening words. Colin, her husband told Mrs Thatcher that he had some very interesting suggestions to put to her which he thought would be useful politically. Mrs Thatcher invited him to see her at 10 Downing Street and set aside a period of 15 minutes of her busy time. Pauline wrote out his remarks and then said she would give Colin the answers to the questions that Mrs Thatcher would ask. Mrs Thatcher did just that and Colin read out the answers that Pauline had given him. Eventually Mrs Thatcher realised what was happening and asked Colin how he knew the questions she would ask. He told her that his wife had anticipated everything and had written it all down to make it easy for him. Mrs Thatcher was more than impressed and said she would give his suggestions full consideration. She 'sat' on her legs on her settee and the interview lasted one hour.

On another occasion Pauline and her husband visited South America to see the wonderful Inca town of Machu Pichu. When she entered the ancient area of the town buildings, she suddenly began to see the whole area as it was in the distant past – complete with the people, dogs etc.

Her barrister sister had warned her never to give witness in a court of law because of these many strange visions.

The case of Gerad Varley (6.06.78)

This man had heard about our healing because his family were in business in Sheffield as Military tailors and he visited fairly often from his normal home in Berkshire. He was suffering from severe sciatica in both legs. It was probably caused by his job as an oil sale representative for one of the big companies. He had to travel about 55,000 miles a year to petrol stations throughout the country. He walked with a very pronounced heel and toe movement in his efforts to reduce the pain he felt.

I asked him to take a seat on the treatment stool and gave healing to the lower back area. In a very short time he said he could hardly believe it – but the pain had gone. I suggested that he should try walking around the room, which he did. All pain had disappeared and he expressed surprise and delight. Then he asked if I could give him treatment for Dupuytren's contracture. I told him I did not know what it was but that it was possible to give treatment for anything and everything, and asked him to show me what it was. He extended both hands and there were the signs of trouble. On each hand there was a raised tendon from the wrist towards the space between the little finger and the third finger. I stroked each raised ridge from the wrist down to the base of the finger. To our amazement and his delight, the problems disappeared and his hands became normal.

He wrote me a letter a few days later to confirm the cures had stayed cured.

The case of Betty Waterall   13th October 1982

She came to us for healing having heard of us from mutual friends. She was suffering acutely from the stress of her daughter's murder. Her daughter had broken off her friendship with her boyfriend and he had objected strongly to the separation and to the fact that she had made a new attachment to a new boyfriend.

He had made an entry into their bungalow after her parents had gone early to market (they were butchers with a stall in Sheffield market hall). He had entered her locked bedroom and strangled her while she was still in bed. The police had at first suspected the new boyfriend but the murderer had been caught and charged with her murder. Much to the disgust of the police and the Waterall family, he was given a prison sentence of only 4 years.

When she came for treatment I was influenced to pass my hands slowly down her back. She sighed gently and said "Oh, that feels better" and burst into gentle tears.

Some years later she came to a party I had organised to attend a seminar in Lytham St. Anne's, run by Gordon Higginson, to further her interest in the spirit world. During the last demonstration given by Gordon Higginson to the whole course, he singled out Betty and said, "Your telephone number is 30406 isn't it?" She said it was, and then he said something about her murdered daughter and she burst into tears. He said he was sorry to have caused her any distress and left her to go on to other recipients.

After the demonstration was over I went to find Gordon and told him why Betty had burst into tears, he immediately said "Do bring her to see me before you go, I'm sure I can help her". So I told Betty and she asked me to accompany her as she felt she would be likely to break down again. So I went with her to give her healing and support.

Gordon spoke gently to Betty and explained that he could tell her everything that had happened. He told her straight away that she and her husband had been blaming themselves for not keeping her bedroom door locked – but he told her that her ex-boyfriend had got a key to this door and had been able to enter the bedroom. He then told her everything about the room and the views from the window; also the furniture and decorative articles on the dressing table and window sills. Then he told her that the bedclothes were covered in blood and Betty said this was true but that she could ignore the blood stains as they were used to blood, being butchers.

Gordon then gave her some personal messages from her daughter which made her feel quite differently and we came away with a much greater appreciation of Gordon's remarkable gifts.

Letter of Acknowledgement

Cookham Dean
Berkshire
13.06.78

Dear Alan
May I first of all thank you and Joyce for curtailing your evening to help a stranger, and at such short notice.
I felt terribly embarrassed when Gill told me of the arrangements. However, all that I can say is a very sincere thank you for all your kindness and help, which I do appreciate.

I think that my back trouble may take time and may require more than one period of treatment. Possibly the delay in recovery is self inflicted, due to all the driving and sitting that I do in the normal course of business. However, I have felt more relaxed over the last few days, and have even attempted a little gardening and chipping practice in the field adjacent to my home.

I do not cease to be amazed at the difference to both my hands. Whilst 'Dupitroums' are still in evidence in both hands, the discolouration has disappeared and the disfigurement has almost gone. I do not think that I would have believed it, had I not experienced it. I can move both hands much more freely; it is a lovely feeling.

It may be that one more session would be all that would be needed to complete your work. I recall that you felt your powers were spent when you were treating my hands; understandably so after such a long, concentrated period of effort. However, I would say again, the improvement is significant.

I enquired of my parents this morning, how their dog Bella was progressing. Unfortunately they haven't noticed any change in the hind leg limping, but they think that the dog is out of pain, so that is good news.

I do not know when I shall next be in the Sheffield area, but I would be most grateful if I could call again to see you, and if the dog is still the same perhaps I could bring her too.

By the way the specialist that I saw for the other "little" problem was a 'urological' surgeon.

I enclose a small contribution towards your new centre. Again many thanks.

Yours sincerely,

Gerard Varley.

Kenneth Wilson, farmer – and the case of the stolen ewe and lamb

Ken first came to me in the mid 1980's. First, I think with an aging sheep dog of which he was very fond. Its back legs were collapsing out of control. He lifted it out of the rear of his Land Rover and I gave it treatment to its pelvic area and spine. After the healing had stopped the dog jumped back into the vehicle, much to Ken's amazement.

He came to me for treatment for himself in 1986 and onwards with various complaints. He obviously benefited, and in 1992 his wife, Angela, also came for treatment. In 1992 he had a serious accident with his tractor. This affected his left leg, knee and left thumb; right arm, shoulder, lower ribs etc. General healing helped greatly in the recovery. There were many visits throughout the 1990's then one day in the spring of 1996 he rang me with a strange request.

He said 'I know you have some strange powers and I am wondering if you can help me recover some stolen sheep and lambs?' They had been put into a field some way from the farmhouse. The field was just above the Millstone Inn on the Sheffield road out of Hathersage. The field itself was enclosed by good stone walls, with wire posts, wire netting and a locked gate. He rang me on a Monday morning to tell me that one ewe and her two lambs were missing, and they could not have got out by any natural means. Naturally, I said that I and my 'circle' would try to help.

This we did at once and Joyce came up with 'seeing' a small white van parked against the field wall very early in the morning of Monday. She 'saw' two men and then the van going south through Chatsworth park. A very similar result came from Gladys. So I said that we must now resort to mind control methods (my term). And proceeded to send out the message to the unknown men that what they had done was both wrong, and without much profit, and full of risks to them of discovery. That they should immediately bring them back under cover of darkness and put them back where they had found them. On the following Thursday Ken rang me to say, 'They are back'. (It should be mentioned that a lady helper who lived near the Millstone, had in fact seen a white van near the field on the Monday morning when she had to get up in the early hours when she felt unwell).

I discovered that Ken wrote poetry: Here are some examples of his work.

MEG, My faithful collie

I well remember years ago
When you were a little pup
You couldn't jump upon my knee
So I had to lift you up

You licked my hair, you licked my face
As you sat upon my lap
In your mischievous, loving way
You tried to snatch my cap

A ball of furry bouncing fun
That was you alright

Tiny paws and tiny ears
And eyes that shone so bright

Growing up was never dull
You loved trying to round up sheep
When you thought you'd done enough
Off you went to sleep

When you began your working life
You did as you were told
You gathered in my ovine friends
And put them in the fold

When blizzards raged one stormy night
The snow blew in your face
You helped me drive some four score sheep
To a safe and sheltered place

I often think about that night
Just you and me together
Upon those wild and lonely moors
You withstood the treacherous weather

With a smile on your face and a wag of the tail
You were always there when I needed aid
At break of dawn at lambing time
Just one of the memories that will never fade

Throughout your life of thirteen years
You were my faithful friend
A friend who never let me down
Ever faithful to the end

Now you are with the Good Shepherd above
Your spirit running free
Among the hills of paradise
Around a tranquil sea

Life on earth is very brief
But we forged a lasting bond
A bond of friendship that can never break
Even in the life beyond

Ken Wilson

A Summer's Day

Summer, Glorious Summer
With all its radiant charm
A million colours greet the eye
To make our thoughts more calm

Dawn chorus heralds the new born day
A beautiful symphony in the morning sky
Every note of every chord
To my senses gently fly

The morning sun with all its power
Burns off the valley mist
Rays of warmth descend to earth
And every flower is kissed

Butterflies on the buddleia feed
A host of fluttering wings
Each sip of nectar that they take
To them much pleasure brings

Swallows in great skilful flight
Swoop low to catch their prey
With lightening speed they twist and turn
As though in giddy play

A row of fledgling birds arrayed
On top of the garden wall
With ruffled plumage not yet preened
They respond to mother's call

Off they fly with tiny wings
To perch in a sycamore tree
Perhaps it's good I do not know
What will be their destiny

In verdant pastures all around
Sheep and cattle seek the shade
Beneath a tree or tall old hedge
Or in a sheltered glade

Honey bees hum in the heat of the day
And into nasturtium trumpets creep
They do not move or make a sound
As though in peaceful sleep

Pussy stretched out taking rest
Under a lilac tree
Her only thoughts that I would guess
What will there be for tea

Fields of waving, ripening grass
Very soon will be the day
When man, machine and nature
Bring forth the smell of new mown hay

In garden, woodland, field alike
An exquisite scent pervades the air
No man should ever want for more
The delights of summer everywhere

Now the day begins to close
When evening shadows fall
Gone are the sounds of birds and bees
Nature's peace lies over all

The setting sun rests on a hill
Like a ball of crimson fire
All the things I've seen today
Have filled my hearts desire

Ken Wilson

The Bluebell Wood

How wonderful is nature's poem
It portrays such beautiful things
Like the sighing of trees at dead of night
Or the twirl of a butterfly's wing

If you sit quite still in woodland bower
The wonders of nature never cease
You can hear a hundred different notes
If you put your mind at peace

Little bird sing forth your song
Your audience is but one
You I'll applaud with all my heart
Till every note has gone

The mistle thrush with her melodious twitter
Aloft a tiny tree
The sweetest music to my ears
Every chord in harmony

Rippling, ever rippling
The stream meanders on its way
Beneath its bank so rarely seen
Countless moths at play

Where ferns spread out their sinewy fronds
This quiet place I know so well
Not often seen by the human eye
Where myriad insects dwell

In bluebell wood where oft I go
Bathed in the morning dew
All around me God has made
A million bells of blue

He has given me sight to see
 Why should I crave for more?
Enter nature's lovely house
And open every door

Ken Wilson

A Robin

When winter spreads her icy wings
From lofty branch the storm cock sings
The leaves are gone, the trees are bare
Snow flakes scurry through the bitter air

The ground is hard no footsteps mark
No sound of linnet or of lark
Very soon a sheet of white
Will cover all within our sight

Throughout the night the blizzards rage
The trees bend o'er as if with age
Gone are the fields of green and brown
Nature is dressed in pure white gown

Morning comes we look outside
God has spread His mantle wide
The wind has ceased the snow now gently falls
On the farmyard gate a hungry robin calls

He's had no warm and cosy bed
No soft pillow to lay his head
He's survived the night that's all that matters
With hearty voice he gaily chatters

We give him food he takes the lot
Without a plate it matters not
He hops and plays and flicks his feathers
Seems so happy, endures all weathers

With grateful heart he accepts what's given
Upon this earth he's found his heaven
I'm happy here would be his call
This little bird, is he a lesson to us all

Ken Wilson

The case of Maurice Womersley

He came to us for healing in September 1978. His complaint
was Myasthenia Gravis. He had been referred by his doctor
to a specialist neurologist Mr Gumpert, the doctor son of
Doctor Father who had had a practice at Fulwood in
Sheffield.

Mr Gumpert had decided that Maurice should go into the
Claremont Nursing Home, Sheffield; it had a good reputation
and was staffed by nuns. After a week of tests carried out by
Mr Gumpert, he said he could not come to any firm
conclusions. All of this had cost £500.00 (quite a large sum
in those days). He did not get any better and his wife told
their doctor and Mr Gumpert that she wanted a second
opinion. At this, Mr Gumpert decided that he, Maurice,
should again enter the nursing home and carried out a further
week of tests, again without any decision being arrived at.

Then Mrs Womersley, Maureen, took matters into her own
hands and consulted a London Specialist physician. It was
extraordinary. As Maurice walked into his consulting rooms
the specialist said 'You are suffering from Myasthenia
Gravis'. The symptoms are so very obvious that you do not

need any examination to determine the problem. He said there was a specially developed drug to deal with this disease and I will communicate with your Mr Gumpert and advise him to prescribe it for you immediately.

After some weeks they still had not heard from Mr Gumpert, but the London Specialist called Maurice and asked if he had been prescribed the medicine. When he heard that Mr Gumpert had not done so, he sent the prescription.

He made steady progress with our healing and came on a regular basis. In February 1980 he was sitting on the treatment stool and Joyce was 'looking' for signs etc. when she said there is an Indians face showing on Maurice's chest. It was the well known face of Silver Birch who was the control of Maurice Barbanell, the Jewish editor of the Psychic News. As Maurice had been feeling occasions of breathlessness we took this as a sign that he should have his heart examined. He did and was told that his aortic valve was worn out and would only last a few weeks. So he had the valve replacement operation.

The sighting of Silver Birch was so unusual that I reported it to John Dreghorn the then President of the N.F.S.H. He suggested I write direct to Maurice Barbanell the Editor of the Psychic News. So I did and he acknowledged my letter and said he would ask Silver Birch about it at their next séance. A week or so later he wrote to say Silver Birch had confirmed his VISIT to our healing of Maurice "He had seen our LIGHT and had wanted to help". It gave us great encouragement.

As he was a pig merchant he elected to have a pig's valve rather than a plastic one. He had healing from us and was able to walk back into our house only eight days after the open heart surgery. In December 1982 he came with a frozen shoulder. The doctor told him it would be two years before it would be completely better. With our healing it was OK in ten minutes.

He finally passed away in December 1987 but we were to come across other patients of this Mr Gumpert and always with the same disappointing experience.

Infertility Cases

One of the worst of human deprivations must be that of being childless when both husband and wife want to have a family more than anything else in the world. We have had such expressions of joy when we have been able to help in conception that a few of our cases may be of interest. Sufficient to encourage others to try Spiritual Healing when all else seems to have failed.

It is a long time since we gave our first healing for infertility. It occurred when Peter Schofield, our son John's gardener helper started us off on this course. He was a part-time park ranger and had himself benefitted from healing after falls and physical strains. He asked if this could be of help to his head ranger. They had been married for six years and had not succeeded, although their medical advisors could find nothing wrong with either of them.

Joyce and I saw them together and Joyce 'saw' nothing wrong with the husband, but saw darkness over the ovary areas on the wife. She experienced great heat from my hands and Joyce 'saw' darkness replaced by light blue and finally gold colours to the aura. They conceived and had a fine baby boy. They told their infertile friends and we had a succession of couples for treatment.

One such case concerned a Mrs Hilary Edwards (who gave permission for this disclosure); she had heard of us through a friend whose parents lived nearby and who had also benefitted. This lady was a mid-wife working with Stafford Maternity Hospital. Her trouble was known; she had no fallopian tubes through earlier problems. She was 24 years old and had been married for six years. She had healing in the usual way, over the ovaries, and went home. Not expecting that a miracle could have happened, she also applied to the Steptoe Clinic for IVF treatment.

She was called for examination by this clinic some three months later. She was amazed when they said 'You do not need us, you are already pregnant'. After she had the usual scan at about five months, she phoned to say that the afterbirth was in the wrong position and that this would require a caesarean birth, could she come for a treatment to correct it? So we said yes and she had this extra treatment. A week later she had a further scan by her closely monitoring hospital and was delighted to learn that the afterbirth had moved to its correct position. I had certainly felt movement under my hands at the time of the second healing.

Subsequently she asked the hospital if she was likely to be able to conceive again, as she did not want an only child. They said that her conception was a miracle, a chance in a million and that another would require an even bigger one. Multiply a million by a million. Anyway she had further absent healing and had two more children. Then she asked me to 'stop it' and they had no more

There were many more cases and our tally is now 94 successes, with some results not known (some parents fail to tell us the results of healing, especially when it is successful).

Poems and sayings

The following few poems were all collected and sent to me by a very sweet old lady, who was in her late seventies, and she also sent me a very decorative small box which she had wrapped in a floral paper on to which she had fixed a nosegay of artificial violets. This came through the post and on the front was stuck a printed small poem which was as follows:-

Here is a very special gift,
that you can never see;
the reason it's so special,
It's just for you from me.

Whenever you are lonely,
or feel a little blue;
you only have to hold this gift
to know I think of you.

You never should unwrap it,
leave the ribbon tied;
please hold the box close to your heart,
it's filled with love inside.

So I do not know the names of the poets but her name was Dorothy Emberton.

How old folk are worth a fortune
Old folk are worth a fortune with <u>silver</u> in their hair, <u>gold</u> in their teeth, <u>stones</u> in their kidneys, and <u>lead</u> in their feet and <u>gas</u> in their stomachs.

Call Me a Frivolous Old Girl
I have become more sociable with the passing of the years; some might even call me a frivolous old girl! I'm seeing <u>five gentlemen</u> every day! As soon as I wake, <u>Will Power</u> helps me to get out of bed and then I go to see <u>Jimmy Riddle</u>. Then <u>Charlie Cramp</u> comes along, when he is here he takes up a lot of my time and attention. When he leaves, <u>Arthur Ritis</u> shows up and stays the rest of the day. He doesn't like me to stay in one place for very long and takes me from <u>Joint</u> to <u>Joint</u>. After such a busy day, I'm really tired and glad to go to bed with <u>Ray Dium B!</u>

What a Life!
The Vicar came to see me the other day and said at my age I should be thinking about the <u>hereafter</u>. I told him I do, all the time, no matter where I am – in the lounge, bedroom or kitchen – I ask myself   "What am I <u>here after?</u>"

From Dorothy E.

I'm fine Thank You

There is nothing the matter with me
I'm as healthy as can be
I have arthritis in both my knees
And when I talk I speak with a wheeze
My pulse is weak and my blood is thin
But I'm awfully well for the shape I'm in.

Sleep is denied me night after night
But every morning I find I'm alright
My memory is failing, my head's in a spin
But I'm awfully well for the shape that I'm in.

The moral is this, as my tale I unfold
That for you and me who are growing old
It's better to say "I'm fine" with a grin
Than let folks know the shape we're in.

How do I know that my youth is all spent?
'Cos my get-up-and-go has got-up and went
But I really don't mind when I think with a grin
Of all the grand places my get-up has bin!

Old age is golden, or so it is said
But sometimes I wonder as I climb into bed
With my ears in a drawer and my teeth in a cup
My eyes on the table until I wake up
E'er sleep overtakes me, I say to myself
"Is there anything else I could lay on the shelf"?

I get up each morning and dust off my wits
Then pick up the paper and read the "obits"
If my name is not there, I know I'm not dead
So I have a good breakfast and go back to bed!

Dorothy Emberton.

We are Survivors

(For those privileged to be born before 1940)

We were born before television, before penicillin, polio shots, frozen foods, contact lenses, videos, Frisbees and the Pill. We were before radar, credit cards, split atoms, laser beams and ball point pens; before dishwashers, tumble driers, electric blankets, air conditioning, drip dry clothes … and before man walked on the moon.

We got married first and **then** lived together *(how quaint can you be?)* We thought 'fast food' was what you ate in Lent, a 'Big Mac' was an oversized raincoat and 'crumpet' we had for tea. We existed before house husbands, computer dating, dual careers and when a 'meaningful relationship' meant getting along with cousins and 'sheltered accommodation' was where you waited for a bus.

We were born before day care centres, group homes and disposable nappies. We never heard of FM radio, tape decks, electric typewriters, artificial hearts, word processors, yogurt and young men wearing earrings. For us 'time sharing' meant togetherness, a 'chip' was a piece of wood or fried potato, 'hardware' meant nuts and bolts and 'software' wasn't a word.

Before 1940 'Made in Japan' meant junk, the term 'making out' referred to how you did in your exams, 'stud' was something that fastened a collar to a shirt and 'going all the way' meant staying on a double-decker to the bus depot.

Pizzas, McDonald and instant coffee were unheard of. In our day, cigarette smoking was 'fashionable', 'grass' was mown, 'coke' was kept in the coal house, a 'joint' was a piece of meat you had on Sundays and 'pot' was something you cooked in. 'Rock music' was a grandmother's lullaby, 'Eldorado' was an ice cream, a 'gay' person' was the life and soul of the party and nothing more, while 'aids' just meant beauty treatment or help for someone in trouble.

We who were born before 1940 must be a hardy bunch when you think of the way in which the world has changed and the adjustments we have had to make. No wonder we are so confused and there is a generation gap today, but...

WE HAVE SURVIVED!!

Dorothy E.

Ode to the Owduns
From a Youngerun

We met – we've been married for just a few years
 but we still respect all the old dears.
We've got our telly and our sunken bath
 the toilets seat's warm – no walk up the path.
The Costa del Sol and a Persian rug
 modern pubs – no smoke room or snug.
We can't look back on two World Wars
 and it's quite true – we lock our doors.
I vaguely remember we used to have coal
 making the fire drove you up the pole.
Children still arrive (we forget the pill)
 with State Aid it's a struggle still.
Penicillin and aspirin are the finer drugs
 helping us to get rid of unwanted bugs.
The NHS may not be the greatest
 but the treatment is definitely the latest.
Of course there are thieves – we've got things to steal
 the standard of living is up a great deal.
Those happy Owduns shouldn't moan all day
 perhaps they should show us a better way.
Kindness and caring comes from the heart
 and it must be there from the start.
The 'Milkie' and paper lad are quiet and that's thanks a heap
 at least we have a good nights sleep.
A night at the flicks – are you mad
 they were only good because it was all you had.
The films today are better by far
 and instead of a bus you can now go by car.
Trouble and strife – now that's nothing new

at least these days we know what to do.
The Younguns are now putting in hours
to rescue this threatened planet of ours.
We'll try to cure the illness before it starts
and believe it or not we can now swap hearts.
I'm sorry you're alone, though not shedding tears
you're lucky to have experienced all those years.
I'm glad you've enjoyed it and do not forget
Owdun dear Owdun you have my respect.

Dorothy E.

Join the Club

Just a line to say I'm living,
 though I'm not amongst the dead,
 and I'm getting more forgetful,
 and mixed up in the head.

I've got used to my arthritis,
 to my dentures I'm resigned,
 I can cope with my bi-focals,
 but 'Ye Gods' I miss my mind.

Sometimes I can't remember
 when I'm standing by the stair,
 if I should be going up for something,
 or have I just come down from there.

I'm before the fridge so often
 when my mind is full of doubt,
 now did I put some food away?
 or come to take something out.

If it's not my turn to write my dear
 I hope you won't get sore,
 I may think that I have written
 and don't want to be a bore.

So remember I love you dearly,
 and wish that you lived near,
 and now it's time to post this letter
 and say goodbye my dear.

At last I stand beside that mailbox,
and my face has sure turned red,
instead of posting this to you,
I have opened it instead.

Dorothy E.

This single poem signed "Jane", was through a medium Mavis Pittilla, while in trance from an ex – novice nun who is now in spirit.

Come, take my hand,
Come walk with me, and you will understand.

Come, take my hand,
Come walk with me, please come and be my friend.

For I am real, I'm here,
Link with me, walk with me
Heart to heart, mind to mind,
For there is the treasure of life.

Fear not, for as you walk along the path
My joy will be to stay your hand from fear,
To keep you safe, to watch, to know,
Always shall we be near.

Goodnight.
Jane.

Footprints

One night a man had a dream. He dreamed he was walking along the beach with the LORD. Across the sky flashed scenes from his life. For each scene, he noticed two sets of footprints in the sand, one belonging to him and the other to the LORD. When the last scene of his life flashed before him, he looked back at the footprints in the sand. He noticed that many times along the path of his life there was only one set of footprints. He also noticed that it happened at the very lowest and saddest time in his life. This really bothered him and he questioned the LORD about it. LORD, you said that once I decided to follow you, you'd walk with me all the way. But I have noticed that during the most troublesome times in my life, there is only one set of footprints, I don't understand why when I needed you most you would leave me.

The LORD replied, My Precious, precious child, I love you and I would never leave you. During your time of trial and suffering when you see only one set of footprints, it was then that I carried you.

From NFSH sources